UNDERSTANDING SJÖGREN'S SYNDROME

by

Sue Dauphin

Pixel Press - Tequesta, FL

Dauphin, Susan H., 1928-
    Understanding Sjogren's syndrome / by Sue Dauphin.
    p. cm.
    Includes bibliographical references and index.
    Preassigned LCCN: 93-085164.
    ISBN 0-9620354-2-4

    1. Sjogren's syndrome--Popular works.   I. Title.

RC647.5S5.D38 1993   616.97'8
                                      QBI93-1193

Printed in the United States of America
Library of Congress Card Number: 93-085164
ISBN #0-962354-2-4

Note: The mention or listing of medications, products and treatments in this book does not constitute endorsement by the author or the publisher. The lists are not necessarily comprehensive and there may be other products or medications available that are helpful. The National Sjögren's Syndrome Association maintains and periodically updates more extensive listings.

Table of Contents

Preface: Understanding Sjögren's Syndrome

To readers of *Sjögren's Syndrome: The Sneaky "Arthritis"*, this book may seem like an old friend. Many parts are identical to the original book. After all I didn't set out to rewrite history and some things have not changed. But keep reading. Much has changed and there are many new items added or updated within the earlier text as well as completely new sections.

I had no idea the response to the Sneaky "Arthritis" book would be so great. So many of you wrote to tell me of your experiences with Sjögren's syndrome that when the time came to print more copies, I decided to rework the whole book to include your concerns.

Many of you wrote that the book reflected closely your own symptoms and your need for answers. It was very gratifying to hear that the book helped so many of you. But when I read, "What about malabsorption or chronic fatigue syndrome?" I understood again that Sjögren's syndrome is an exceedingly complex disease.

This is a new edition of *Sjögren's Syndrome: The Sneaky "Arthritis"* greatly expanded and, hopefully, greatly improved. As much as possible, your questions have been addressed and maybe some things you haven't even thought of are included. Even if you have read the original book, read this new one, there's lots that's new. And if it occasionally seems that I am repeating myself, please be patient. Often I have new thoughts on information that was already included in the original book. I hope you will find it all helpful.

Preface: Sjögren's Syndrome: The Sneaky "Arthritis"

Someone you know may be hurting and not know why. He or she belongs to a "chapter" of the reluctant fraternity of an estimated 36 million Americans with arthritis. Worldwide, it's estimated that more than 3% of the population have some type of autoimmune disease. More than 4 million are thought to have Sjögren's syndrome, Most have never been diagnosed. Far too many doctors don't recognize it when they see it.

Patients may go 20 years before getting a diagnosis. Often they are labeled hypochondriacs. Their mouths are dry. There's 'something in their eyes'. Their joints hurt. They get terribly tired. What's more, their teeth hurt. Doctors may blame it on nervous tension, leaving the frustrated patient more confused than ever. These people go to many different doctors for all these pains. So no one doctor hears the whole story. Patients are told it's all in their minds. They are sent to psychiatrists or told to take up a hobby and quit complaining. What a relief it is finally to hear someone say, "Your problems may all be related. You have Sjögren's syndrome." Even there's no cure yet, there are many ways to ease the symptoms of SS.

List of Illustrations

Dedication

Understanding Sjögren's Syndrome is dedicated to the men in my life. First and foremost, my husband Vern has worked lovingly right with me through every step of the way and late into many nights. My son Bill's watchful eye made sure I said what I meant to say and wrote it right.

It's written with particular thanks to all those Sjögren's syndrome patients who have told me *Sjögren's Syndrome: The Sneaky "Arthritis"* has helped. And to Sidney Dorros for his credo, "Accommodation without surrender" which he lived all his life and left as a legacy for all chronic illness patients.

Acknowledgements

Thanks to Drs. Stephen Pflugfelder, David Sullivan, Hans 's-Gravenmade, Robert Fox, Frank Arnett, Harry Moutsopoulos, Stefano Bombardieri, Philip Fox, John Tiffany, Austin Mircheff, Kenichi Yoshino, Gabriel Fernandes, Troy Daniels, and Kasuo Tsubota, for encouraging me and helping to update the work. And to the members of NSSA, especially Harriett Miller.

Thanks also to Dr. Susumu Sugai and his colleagues who translated *Sjögren's Syndrome: The Sneaky "Arthritis"* into Japanese so their patients could read it. In spite of the challenge of translating my sometimes unorthodox phrases, they have agreed to do it again.

UNDERSTANDING SJÖGREN'S SYNDROME:

PART I The "Sneaky" Disease

Chapter 1 - Introduction

"Do you like to eat saltines?"

That simple question was the first in a long series my doctor asked, that led, finally, to a surprise diagnosis. After twenty years of being told I had rheumatoid arthritis (RA), and being treated accordingly, I was sitting in a new rheumatologist's office listening to him describe an ailment I had never heard of.

Sjögren's syndrome, he was telling me, was not actually a single disease, but as its name implies, a collection of symptoms. Symptoms that involved eyes that were always dry, a dry mouth, and the aching joints that inspired the RA diagnosis.

The problems of Sjögren's syndrome are so diverse that they often go unrecognized as having any relation to each other. A patient may, as I did, go to an ophthalmologist for an explanation of blurred vision, a dermatologist about dry and irritated skin, a urologist about recurring infections, and an internist about the aching and swollen joints of arthritis. Dentists and dental technicians constantly admonish her about the buildup of plaque and the excessive cavities that seem to constantly appear in spite of ardent brushing and flossing.

Often, no one, least of all the patient, sees any correlation among all these ailments, and more often than not, the patient ignores or suppresses some symptoms for fear of being considered a hypochondriac. In addition, the symptoms develop at different rates, and surface (or at least become annoying enough to demand attention) at different times in the patient's lifetime.

Early Symptoms

I had always had an aversion to crackers and other dry foods such as the gritty corn bread that is so essential to Southern menus, but I never gave it a thought as a medical problem until the very moment when my doctor asked that deceptively simple question. Different patients report different symptoms as the first sign of trouble. Fabric salesperson Mary Jones'* irritated eyes and blurry vision were laid to the presence of sizing dust in her shop atmosphere. Celeste Johnson's mother reacted to Celeste's frequent "swollen glands" by keeping her home from school for a day and giving her chicken soup. Celeste's cousin John claimed to have had "mumps" three times, once more than the medical maximum.

---

* Some names have been changed to protect confidentiality..

The Author's Story Begins

In my case the first recognizable sign of trouble was swollen and aching elbows and wrists. I remember very well how it started. I had transplanted a whole hedge of shrubs from an abandoned home down the street to my own yard, digging each one up, lifting it into the trunk of my car and reversing the chore at my home. There were at least 20 of the privet type bushes and I was proud of the effect as they all lined up along the edge of my property. The next day, a Saturday, we went out with friends on their boat. They were enthusiastic water-skiers and urged us to try the sport. My husband was instantly good at it but I was never quite able to get up on my feet with the skis firmly set under me. I tried, gamely, a dozen or so times but finally gave up. One reason for my difficulty, which I wouldn't admit to the others, was that my elbows and wrists were hurting more with each try as the tow rope tightened to pull me afloat.

By the following Monday, my knuckles had joined the ranks of the swollen. My aches were severe enough to get me to my family doctor, an internist who gave me an immediate diagnosis. It required only a casual examination of my hands and arms. He noted the bulges on the outer sides of both wrists. "Arthritis," he said. And then because my pain was symmetrical, the same on both sides of my body, he added, "Rheumatoid." So confidant was he of his pronouncement that he said tests, though available, were not necessary.

Thus began a long series of treatments that included Indocin and massive doses of aspirin. I took these consistently for about 10 years, until I developed an ulcer and was told to discontinue all medication. A hot whirlpool, installed in my home at my doctor's prescription, was to be my only concession to the aching joints from then on.

Different Patients, Different Experiences

Other patients had different experiences but with striking similarities. Janet Walker, an elementary school teacher, traces her problems to a common occupational hazard; picking up infections from students. Midway through a particularly trying day of math exercises and science labs, she discovered she had broken out in neck-to-toe spots. Only later did one of her students tell her, "That's what Tammy had!" The eighth grader had contracted a rare childhood virus related to the four rashes of the measles family and Janet picked it up from her. Little Tammy's spots were so seldom seen they were known simply as "the fifth rash". Because another teacher at her school was pregnant, Janet stayed home to be on the safe side. The rash was followed within 24 hours by a still more unwelcome set of symptoms. Janet's hands became swollen and tender, making the simplest tasks painful. Her knees became so inflamed, she couldn't walk. Just getting up from a couch was a stressful task. Opening doors was difficult and dressing herself almost impossible.

Although the fifth rash is not a part of Sjögren's syndrome, hindsight indicates that the trauma of the virus may have triggered Janet's later problems. She only knows the aches never quite left her joints and she just didn't rebound to her former springy level of energy. It was also at this time that she began having eye troubles. Like a television screen in an electric storm, Janet's vision was cluttered with blind patches, zig-zag lines and technicolor flashes. Her eyes were scratchy and irritated. Not until many years later was any connection made between her erratic vision and her painful joints.

Twenty-two year old Charles Swenson tells a different story. He recalls going to his south Texas home for Thanksgiving a couple of years back, hoping his mother wouldn't notice the strange puffiness of his cheeks. Mother did notice, of course, and insisted he see a doctor. The swellings along his jaws had been coming and going for some time for no apparent reason. Friends commented that he had gained (or lost) weight, according to whether his jaws were swollen or not on any given day. He had had mumps as a boy, so he and his mother could only think some kind of infection was behind his chipmunk-like appearance. The holiday over, he went back to his college and set up an appointment with a local general practitioner. The doctor prescribed medication for the sore throat that also bothered Charles, but was hard put to explain the swollen glands. The soreness of Charles' throat subsided, but the puffy pouches remained

After about four months, Charles sought out another doctor who at once suspected Sjögren's syndrome. Although tests gave mixed results, the doctor felt the diagnosis was confirmed and recommended surgery to remove Charles' defective saliva glands. The young student was understandably hesitant about such a drastic step and sought another opinion. This time the testing was extensive and conclusive. He did indeed have Sjögren's syndrome but the new doctors were reluctant to operate, suggesting he postpone that as long as possible. There were ways to deal with his dry mouth in the meantime. He discovered that the red eyes he had been blaming on too much late night studying, were really part of the syndrome and could also be treated. At least Charles now had a diagnosis. He could begin to cope.

Figure 1 Cheeks Like a Chipmunk

Coping was becoming increasingly difficult for Betty Rosen, a suburban wife, mother of three and caregiver for her husband's elderly parents, who were victims of Parkinson's and Alzheimer's diseases. This shouldn't have been too much for her to handle, but she was constantly tired and a variety of problems plagued her. Her eyes became too irritated to tolerate the contact lenses she tried to wear. She repeatedly lost her voice for no apparent reason.

The tiredness progressed to weakness and a "hurt all over feeling." She began using a cane to help her walk. This struck her as unreasonable, since she was only 30 years old. But the doctors she consulted couldn't pinpoint the problem. They told her it was all in her mind. She should see a psychiatrist. "I was falling apart," she says. "They kept saying 'I can't find a thing wrong with you. You'll just have to live with it.'" Then one night, while watching TV, Betty happened to glance at a table lamp in the corner of the room. It looked as if it were smoking. She checked with her husband but he saw nothing amiss. She kept looking and the lamp kept "smoking". And there were "halos" all around the light. She tried to ignore the problem but the halos wouldn't go away so she finally went to an ophthalmologist. He thought perhaps her eyes were prematurely aging, but could give no reason for it.

Betty did try going to a psychiatrist. She stuck with that for five years and says it helped emotionally, but did nothing to solve her physical problems. Prayer, she says, also helped her get through these times. But the halos still would not go away and walking became even more difficult. She went to 19 doctors during this period. But each one looked at a different aspect of her situation. In a familiar pattern, she saw an ophthalmologist, an internist, an orthopedist, and a bone and muscle specialist, among others. Finally, she saw an internist who took a different approach. He made it a challenge to identify her problem. Betty wrote down everything that was wrong with her. The list covered "a huge page and it was tiny, tiny handwriting." The doctor came to the conclusion she had lupus, or if not, some other connective tissue disease. Her blood tests were always just slightly off the norm, but not enough so to make a firm diagnosis. Things came to a head when she began falling down with no warning. "I'd just topple over as if someone had turned my key off." The internist sent Betty to a muscle specialist who, familiar with Sjögren's syndrome, was able finally to connect all the dots in Betty's clinical records. He told her she had Sjögren's syndrome, secondary to dermatomyositis, a form of connective tissue disease that attacks muscles. The extraordinary weakness of Betty's legs was at last explained and she was able to begin treatment. For Betty Rosen, the road to diagnosis had taken six years.

My journey was longer, perhaps because it began earlier; when the awareness of Sjögren's syndrome was even less widespread than it is now. With treatment, my ulcer healed, but the aching of the joints persisted. I faithfully continued to take two baths per day in my hot tub. The fact that my skin became progressively drier seemed only a small price to be paid for the soothing effects of the baths. But those effects were short-lived and the pain would inevitably return soon after the towel finished its work. What's more, new problems appeared. Knees, hips and back chimed in to let me know all was not well. When I complained to my doctor, he told me I would simply have to choose between putting up with my aches, or ruining my stomach.

About that time I decided to look elsewhere for medical care. My new doctor, a general practitioner, helped me begin a search for a suitable treatment, using an NSAID (non-steroidal anti-inflammatory drug).

The list of drugs we tried would read like a pharmacist's order list. Fortunately, there is a wide assortment of these anti-inflammatory agents to choose from. Most arthritis patients are familiar with them through this same process of selection to find the one that is effective for them. It would seem at first that I was tolerating the drug, and the relief from the pains was indeed pleasant. But soon the familiar burning sensation would begin in my stomach and I would know that particular drug was not for me.

Meanwhile, I saw several eye doctors about the blurry mucus I couldn't seem to clear out of my eyes. And I suffered increasing allergic reactions to multiple or unidentified substances. After one particularly severe episode, which was blamed on one of the NSAIDs I tried, I was started on the corticosteroid, prednisone. When my rash subsided I cut way down but continued a low dosage of the popular cortisone drug. A later skin rash brought me to an allergist who expressed dismay at my long-term use of cortisone and told me some of the possible side effects I had not known about. (The side effects of cortisone and other drugs will be discussed in Chapter 5.) It was this concern that finally inspired me to seek out the specialized help of the rheumatologist who finally labeled my Sjögren's syndrome.

Sjögren's Syndrome Defined

What do all the patients we've talked about have in common? A lot of things. But the thing that stands out most sharply in all the stories is the multiplicity of their symptoms and the resulting difficulty of diagnosis. The problems they have stem from the fact that the disease has long been considered rare, and until recently was given short shrift in medical schools. A doctor in his 40s or older would probably have heard Sjögren's mentioned only briefly during his student days. He was probably told that he was not likely to see actual cases during his regular practice. Younger doctors now training receive much more information and are therefore more aware of it, especially in those disciplines affected by the syndrome. Thus it is still possible for patients to go to many doctors who, quite innocently, fail to correlate the symptoms described. Additionally, because of the overlapping nature of many of Sjögren's symptoms, it is often hard to distinguish between Sjögren's and rheumatoid arthritis or lupus. According to Dr. Frank Arnett, Director of the Rheumatology Division of the University of Texas Health Science Center in Houston. and a leading Sjögren's researcher, "The borders are blurred, even for the experts. We have pretty well separated RA and Sjögren's, but lupus is more difficult. The serious research into SS only really began in the '80s."

As my doctor informed me, the common symptoms, those necessary for a clinical diagnosis of Sjögren's syndrome, are dry eyes, dry mouth, and aching joints. Any two of these are enough to qualify a patient as having Sjögren's syndrome. In this simple form, it is known as Primary Sjögren's syndrome. This means Sjögren's syndrome without one of an assortment of the connective tissue diseases, such as rheumatoid arthritis, that often accompany SS. Others include lupus (systemic lupus erythematosus or SLE), scleroderma, polymyositis, and dermatomyositis. All of these are disorders that occur when the body's immune system turns against us. Cells in the bloodstream designed to protect us from invading germs and disease organisms become "confused" and attack our own tissues, instead of the enemy. The type of cells doing the attacking and the type of tissue under siege define the disease. In the case of Sjögren's syndrome, the body's exocrine glands, particularly the tear glands and the salivary glands, are the victims of marauding cells from the bloodstream that invade the glands and prevent them from producing the fluids that lubricate the eyes or mouth. As is obvious from our case stories, other organs can be — and usually are — involved. These, as well as the related connective tissue diseases of secondary Sjögren's syndrome, their treatment, and the outlook for the future will be discussed further in later chapters. From the many letters I have received from Sjögren's patients all over the country, and in fact all over the world, as a response to the first edition of this book, I have learned even more of the great variety of manifestations of the disease. I will quote from these experiences throughout the book to illustrate the problems encountered by typical SS victims. I don't want to add to the worries of those who might have Sjögren's syndrome; rather, I want to increase the general awareness of the condition so many more people may identify the source of their annoying problems, and begin, as our cases have, to cope. And to let the people involved know they are definitely not alone.

A Chronic Autoimmune Disease

Sjögren's syndrome is a chronic systemic autoimmune disease, in which the immune system, the body's network of defense mechanisms, reacts against itself. A certain type of lymphocyte, a white blood corpuscle that circulates in the blood and lymph systems, normally mobilizes to fight off infections and foreign bodies. These cells produce the antibodies that give us immunity to diseases once conquered, such as measles. But sometimes some of them turn against the very body they are supposed to protect. They infiltrate and damage exocrine (mucus-secreting) glands as if _they_ were foreign bodies. The injured glands are no longer able to lubricate our mouths, eyes, joints and other parts of our bodies.

Secondary SS

When the familiar triad of symptoms is present along with one of several connective tissue diseases, it is considered secondary Sjögren's syndrome. Probably as many as one quarter of all people with rheumatoid arthritis also have Sjögren's syndrome. They are most often the ones who don't know of their SS because the arthritis symptoms demand much more attention. In fact, it might be 40 years from the time RA is diagnosed to the time the first symptoms of Sjögren's syndrome are recognized.

Some Surprising Numbers

For many years Sjögren's syndrome has been considered a rare disease, but doctors and researchers are becoming more and more convinced it has been seriously underrated. However, because of the lack of documented cases, and because so many people go undiagnosed, there is great confusion, even among the experts, as to how common the disease really is. As early as 1971,

Martin A. Shearn [1] estimated that SS "affects an estimated 2% of the population." He pointed out that "the frequency with which it is recognized depends in large measure on the frame of reference and the awareness of the physician who initially sees the patient." He mentions a patient who had been seen 22 times by ophthalmologists for "chronic conjunctivitis" before anyone thought of SS. Various doctors have made educated guesses based on the number of rheumatoid arthritis (RA) patients they have seen who also have KCS (keratoconjunctivitis sicca). Naturally, this brings differing results, but the number of RA patients who also have SS ranges from 30 to 50 percent. Dr. Norman Talal, [2] in 1984 calculates that if 25 percent of the nation's 8 million RA patients have SS and an equal number have SS without RA, there must be at least 4 million SS sufferers, many as yet undetected. Another statistic says that every year, a million people will be told for the first time that they have arthritis. How many of those will have SS along with or instead of their arthritis is almost impossible to guess, but estimates say 30 to 50% of SS patients also have RA; 5 to 8%, scleroderma; 4 to 5%, lupus.

Probably second only to RA among autoimmune diseases in frequency, SS is found among men and women of all ages, but over ninety percent of patients are women, usually middle aged and white. Still, studies have been made of groups of children, even as young as two and a half years old, with SS.[3] Although SS is often

---

[1] Martin. Shearn, *Sjögren's Syndrome* (Philadelphia:W. B. Saunders, 1971)

[2] Norman Talal, "How to Recognise and Treat Sjögren's Syndrome" *Drug Therapy*, June 1984: 80-87

[3] Chudwin et al "Spectrum of Sjögren's Syndrome in Children" *The Journal of Pediatrics* February 1981; 98:212-217

spoken of as a disease of post-menopausal women, the actual age figures may not bear that out. Sjögren, him-

96% FEMALE
4% MALE

Figure 2 Over 90% of SS patients are women

self, in 1951, charted the ages of his cases (73) along with other cases and found that 142 out of a total of 224 women (more than half) were under the age of 50. Well over one fourth were under 40.[4]

The disease for children turned out to be similar to that of the adults. This also proven true when comparisons were made between men and women patients. No significant differences were noted in age, racial distribution, onset, and length of disease or symptoms, except that men were more likely to have extra complications as opposed to the glandular syndrome alone. Differences noted in blood chemistry have led investigators to look into a possible connection of sex hormones similar to that already accepted in lupus.[5]

---

[4]Henrik Sjögren *Acta Ophthalmologica* 29:33-47, 1951
[5]Rolf Manthorpe, et al "Sjögren's Syndrome: A Review with Emphasis on Immunological Features" *Allergy* 1981; 36: 139-153 *Scandinavian Journal of Rheumatology* 1986; Suppl. 61: 237

In considering the occurrence of SS in children, and the long lead time for diagnosis in some cases, it's interesting that many adults, once they have been diagnosed as having SS, will remember details from their younger years that seem to fit right in. Rose Thomas says, "My husband reminds me that I have had various symptoms for many years prior to the 1982 visits to the doctor." Another correspondent told me she had lost all her teeth at age 22. With some surprise, she wondered if that loss could have been connected with SS. Some may have other problems such as chronic thyroid, kidney, or liver conditions. One older patient remembers having irritated eyes all through his school years. The mean time lag between the actual beginnings of the disease and its identification is eight years, but many, as we have seen, go twenty years or longer in the dark as to the real nature of their illness. This book is intended to help avoid that for as many of those people as possible. And to help us get a fix on what Sjögren's syndrome is all about.

In these days of trillion dollar deficits and billion dollar lawsuits, it is becoming increasingly difficult to grasp the significance of statistics such as those I've been quoting. We can gleefully mimic Carl Sagan with his 'billyuns and billyuns' of stars, but we can only see an infinitesimal part of them. I once read that the human brain can deal with only five units at a time. After that we must start making notes. Or counting on our fingers.

To make it easier for us to understand the scope of SS, I'm going to dream up a mythical city with a population of 50 thousand. That's a more manageable number to handle. We'll call it Sicca City ('sicca' being the

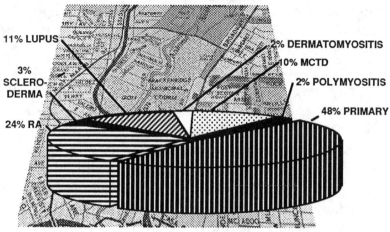

SICCA CITY In the State of Poor-Health

11% LUPUS

3% SCLERO-DERMA

24% RA

2% DERMATOMYOSITIS

10% MCTD

2% POLYMYOSITIS

48% PRIMARY

Figure 3 Sjögren's Patients in Sicca City

medical term for dryness) and, if you'll forgive me, locate it in the state of Poor Health. Of the 50 thousand men, women and children who live there, we can guess that one thousand will have Sjögren's syndrome. Nine hundred of them are women. Approximately 390 of them also have rheumatoid arthritis, 60 have scleroderma, 40 have lupus, and a few have other tissue diseases like dermatomyositis, and polymyositis The remaining 500 have SS alone (primary Sjögren's syndrome) Remember our Sicca Citians as we consider all the aspects of SS, and try by that means to keep it all in perspective.

Chapter 2 - Symptoms

Primary Sjögren's Syndrome
(Sicca Complex)

Once you are diagnosed as having Sjögren's syndrome, your doctor will probably put you into one of Sjögren's two distinct groups. He will say you have Primary Sjögren's syndrome or Secondary Sjögren's syndrome. This will depend on whether you also have one of the rheumatic diseases. If you have dry eyes, dry mouth, and joint pains; or any two of these without any rheumatic diseases (rheumatoid arthritis, lupus, etc.), you have primary Sjögren's syndrome. It is often referred to as sicca complex. "Sicca", which comes from the Latin word siccus (dry), refers to the fact that dryness is the most obvious symptom. There are some significant differences between the two levels of the syndrome, which will be discussed at the end of this chapter.

Dry Eyes (Keratoconjunctivitis Sicca)

Actually the first thing you might notice about your eyes could be the kind of thick, gooey secretion that bothered me. It floats annoyingly around in your eyes. Your vision is obscured and you can't quite wipe the mess away. But its an intermittent nuisance that will go away all on it's own after a while and seems always to be gone when you tell your ophthalmologist about it. "How can I tell you what it is when I see nothing there?" is a common reaction. This gooeyness, surprisingly, can be the result of the lack of tears as the glands try to compensate. All of our five hundred Sicca Citians with primary SS have dry eyes and most of the secondary patients do too, as this, along with the dry mouth, is the hallmark of SS.

In Sjögren's syndrome, white blood cells (lymphocytes) invade the tear glands above and outside the eye (lacrimal) and the smaller glands (meibomian) at the edge of the eyelid.

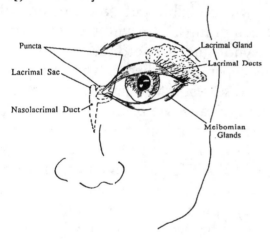

Figure 4 **Tear Ducts and Glands**

The meibomian glands produce the thin, oily outermost layer of the tear film while the watery tears we are familiar with are secreted by the lacrimal gland. Still another layer lies closest to the eyeball. This one is made up of mucus and helps spread the tears evenly over the eye as well as serving as a kind of glue to hold all that moisture in.[6]

When Sjögren's syndrome attacks, the invading cells cause the tissue of the tear (lacrimal) glands to become

---

[6]American Academy of Ophthalmology *Floaters and Flashers* Pamphlet; 1985

fibery and dry, interfering with the glands' ability to make tears.

Without its normally soothing and protective bath of tears, the eye becomes subject to assault from particles of dust and even the grating of its own lid moving against the dry surface of the eyeball. Ohioan

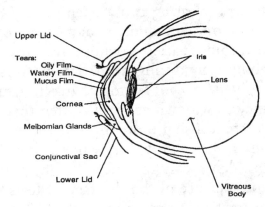

Figure 5 Eyeball With 3-Layer Tear Film

Bernice Kapalin says her eyes are so dry she "can HEAR them opening and closing." Depending on the amount of damage to the gland, the eye marshals what's left of its ability to protect itself and a filmy blurriness occurs. This comes from the buildup of an abnormal type of mucus that works "like an oil spot on a car's windshield." The watery tears that are still available will not cling over the mucus and vision is obstructed.[7] Other complaints include grittiness, a scratchy feeling, or the sensation of something foreign in the eye. Certain patients have written that they have been bothered with protein deposits on contacts and the appearance of halos around street lights. Keratoconjunctivitis also shows up as redness, burning, itching, and extra sensitivity to light (photosensitivity). The eyes feel tired and vision may be less sharp than normal. Since emotional tears

[7]Herbert Kaufman *Keratitis Sicca* International Ophthalmological Clinic; Summer 1984; 24... 133-43

are a different sort from these protective ones, the ability to cry from sadness or anger may or may not be affected. Wearing contact lenses may be ruled out by the irritation. The dryness may be more noticeable at night for some patients whose lids may not always close completely during sleep. The doctors call this *nocturnal lagophthalmos*. To top that off, actual tear production may slow down at night. Often these symptoms are not severe, causing more of a nuisance and discomfort than any real disability, but without proper care, more serious problems can follow. The most likely and obvious consequence of the shortage of tears is corneal abrasion, or scratching. Irritation of the blood vessels (vasculitis) is possible, as is clouding of the cornea (opacity).[8,9]

Having started this book telling the experiences of two SS patients who experienced flashes and "zig-zags" of light that disturbed their vision, it is important to discuss these problems here. The normal aging process involves shrinkage of the gelatin-like substance (vitreous humor) that fills the inside of the eyeball. Many of us, at any age, have seen specks or bits of "debris" that appear to float in front of our eyes. Actually they are inside our eyes, in the vitreous humor. Called floaters, they are small clumps of the gel itself, and they have an annoying way of drifting off when we try to look at them. This is because they are just off center and move with the eye as we try to focus. Annoying as they may be, these floaters are unimportant and may safely be ignored. If floaters get in the way of whatever you are trying to see, the American Academy of Ophthalmology suggests you move your eye around, look-

[8]I. Udell *Dry Eye (Keratitis Sicca)* /Steven Carsons *Sjögren's Syndrome: Distinguishing Primary from Secondary* Ed Great Neck NY, SSFoundation; March 10, 1987
[9]Talal, "How to Recognise and Treat Sjögren's Syndrome", 80-87

ing quickly up and down to shake the floaters into a different position. As we grow older, a much more disturbing thing can happen. We may suddenly see many new floaters at once or flashes of light that persist with no relation to the actual light around us. Although these too, are probably normal changes as part of the aging process, a visit to the ophthalmologist is in order. The lights are most likely the result of minor tears in the retina as the shrinking gel pulls away from it. They will disappear in about a month. But it's possible that a retinal detachment could occur and it is also possible, though apparently uncommon, that the flashes could be caused by inflammation, our old nemesis of SS. For this reason an examination by an ophthalmologist is essential to make sure the problem *is* minor.[10]

Dry Mouth (Xerostomia)

The second major symptom of Sjögren's syndrome is a dry mouth, caused by the lymphocytes attacking their own host, your body. This time their target is the salivary glands, those that supply you with saliva. They become tough and stringy, and unable to generate enough saliva to moisten your mouth. This causes an assortment of uncomfortable problems. The most noticeable, perhaps, is that with little or no lubrication of the teeth and gums, things stick to them. Food attaches itself to your teeth and refuses to slide away as it should. Ordinary chewing gum and chewy candies are likely to be the first things you'll eliminate from your diet just because they're too much trouble. We will see later that

---

[10] American Academy of Ophthalmology *Dry Eye/Understanding Your Condition* Pamphlet; 1985

these items are especially harmful to the Sjögren's syndrome patient. Lettuce, while healthy for the diet, has a distressing tendency to cling to the teeth. Here's where the question of saltines and bread becomes important. They not only stick to your molars, but they give you trouble all the way down, forming dry lumps that are hard to swallow. One doctor in Mexico, Dr. Guillermo J. Ruiz-Arguelles even suggests that tell-tale lipstick smears on the teeth be taken as a warning to investigate the possibility that the patient may have Sjögren's syndrome.[11]

Rampant Tooth Decay

But there is a serious side to this effect. Normally saliva serves as a protective coating for the teeth. It contains ingredients that limit the growth of the bacteria that cause tooth decay, and it bathes the teeth in protective minerals such as calcium, phosphorus, and fluoride.[12] This remineralizes them, replacing lost traces of these essential minerals. Of course, it is obvious that the flow of saliva over the surfaces of the teeth helps to keep them clean, washing away the food particles in between brushings. When this marvelous fluid is in short supply, or missing entirely, it's easy to see what the consequences can be. Food scraps do not get washed away and, in fact, bits and pieces of that mid-afternoon snack adhere firmly. Bacteria have a field day, growing at their own, unrestricted pace. The reservoir

---

[11]G. Ruiz-Arguelles "The "Lipstick-on-Teeth" sign in Sjögren's Syndrome" *New England Journal of Medicine* Oct. 16, 1986; 315: 16
[12]National Institute of Dental Research *Dry Mouth (Xerostomia)* Pamphlet Bethesda MD

of minerals (calcium, phosphorus and fluoride) is depleted and not available for the day-to-day healing the average person enjoys. The teeth are left defenseless against the assaults of acids in such foods as citrus fruits. The infamous plaque that television advertisements warn us against builds up rapidly. It contains more bacteria and is harder to remove. Cavities abound and your teeth are in real danger from decay. My husband used to complain that I had "teeth like butter." The world said I had a "sweet tooth" and ate too much candy. So aside from all the pain of toothaches, and the inconvenience of frequent trips to the dentist, the Sjögren's syndrome victim lives with guilty feelings that the dental problems are all his or her fault. I preferred to blame my troubles on an early dentist who discouraged my mother from having my teeth straightened with braces when I was a child. In those days the straightening would have cost $300 and he told her it wasn't worth it. Now, just capping one of those crooked teeth costs more than that. But poor, long abused Dr. Weston no longer must bear all the blame for my decimated teeth.

Thirst and Throat Problems

The dryness caused by lack of saliva extends, naturally, beyond just its effects on the teeth. The entire mouth needs lubrication and doesn't get it. Factors in the saliva meant to lubricate food are missing. The enzymes that should be in the saliva to start dissolving the food and give the digestive process a boost are decreased or not there at all. The result is difficulty in swallowing. You feel the sensation of a lump in your throat that can even be painful at times and the discomfort can go through.[13] On top of that, the soft tissues of the mouth are dry, making you thirsty much of the time. Sara Endress had the frightening experience of waking up in the middle of the night, with a choking sensation, as if her throat were totally closed. The surface of the tongue may be irritated, split, and sensitive to heat, cold, and peppery foods. Lips and corners of the mouth may crack and be sore and there may be ulcers inside the mouth. Many people complain of a burning sensation in the mouth[14] All these problems leave your mouth susceptible to infections. The dryness provides a particularly favorable climate for yeast infections (most commonly candidiasis) to grow.[15] To add insult to injury, the ability to enjoy the taste of sweet, sour, salty, or bitter foods can be diminished, although some of us who have diet problems might consider that a blessing! Apparently the reduction in saliva brings about a corresponding reduction in the number of taste buds, and then makes matters worse by dampening the tasting ability of the ones that are left.[16] Tasting depends on the presence of saliva, which dissolves taste molecules and carries them to taste receptor cells and also influences the ionic balance of the fluids affecting the cells within the taste buds.[17]

---

[13]G. Kjellen et al "Esophageal Function, Radiography, and Dysphagis in Sjögren's Syndrome" *Digestive Diseases and Sciences;* March 1986; 31: 225-229

[14]S. H. Constantopolos, E. V. Tsianos and H. M. Moutsopoulos Pulmonary and Gastrointestinal Manifestations of Sjögren's Syndrome" *Rheumatic Disease Clinics of North America* Vol. 18, # 3 August 1992 p624

[15]Yvonne L. Hernandez, and Troy Daniels "Oral Candidiasis in Sjögren's Syndrome: Prevalence, Clinical Correlations, and Treatment" *Oral Surgery, Oral Medicine, Oral Pathology* Sep. 1989 ; 68(3) pp324-329

[16]R. I. Henkin et al Abnormalities of Taste and Smell in Sjögren's Syndrome *Annals of Internal Medicine;* 1972; 76: 375-383

[17]Andrew I. Spielman, David B. Kriser "Interaction of Saliva and Taste" *The Journal of Dental Research* 1990; 69: 838-843

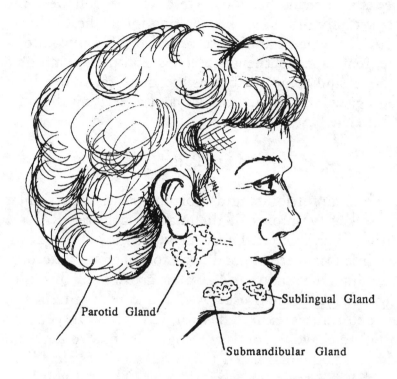

Parotid Gland

Sublingual Gland

Submandibular Gland

Figure 6 Salivary Glands

Because Sjögren's syndrome is an inflammatory process, a painful swelling of the affected glands is all too often a part of the syndrome. In particular, the parotid glands around the mouth may become enlarged. Many Sjögren's syndrome patients have parotid glands that swell repeatedly, as Charles Swenson's did. The jaws may puff out separately or both at the same time, and feel tender, red, and feverish. It can happen suddenly and subside just as swiftly. They seldom become infected, but a hard or lumpy gland could signify a tumor and should be investigated. Helen Ruhl of Detroit, says her swollen cheeks that made her look like a kewpie doll were the first symptom that sent her looking for medical help.

If all this is beginning to sound terribly uncomfortable, remember that few people have all these symptoms at once, and some symptoms are quite rare. And keep reading; we will discuss the ways of alleviating the ones you do have.

Joint Pain

The painful joints and morning stiffness so similar to the key symptoms of rheumatoid arthritis (RA) are partly responsible for the frequent mix-ups in diagnosis. But, in a rare piece of good news for Sjögren's syndrome sufferers, the pain and inflammation of primary Sjögren's syndrome is usually mild and seldom results in the deformities expected with RA. And, if you are going to have secondary Sjögren's syndrome, you usually get the associated tissue disease (RA, etc.) first, and the SS symptoms show up later. Thus, if you have primary SS, you are unlikely to develop the RA later.

With primary SS, the joints most often hurting are the small ones, and the pain comes and goes. The joint pain is symmetrical, as it is in RA; that is, it will usually affect both sides of the body at the same time. Aileen Lull's troubles began in her ankles. Her doctor called it sprains and sent her to a psychiatrist when she refused to accept that.

If your right wrist hurts, chances are the left one does too. When the right knee complains, the left knee is heard from at the same time. The joints may be swollen and warm. The inflammation occurs when the lubricating sheath (synovial capsule) that protects the joint is dried up and nonfunctional. You may often be stiff first thing in the morning, but this generally lasts only a short time. If you get up and go about your normal business, the stiffness will usually fade away in a half hour or so.

Other Exocrine Glands

The glands of the eyes and mouth (tear glands and salivary glands) are part of a system designed to lubricate the various organs throughout the body. Known as exocrine glands, they secrete fluids or mucus to cushion the friction of tissue upon tissue or smooth the way for a particular organ to carry out its appointed function. Exocrine glands are also found in the nasal passages, the lower respiratory system, the digestive tract, the vaginal area, and the skin.

The Respiratory System

Mucous glands line the walls of the larynx (voice box), and the esophagus (the tubes that carry food to the stomach and air to the lungs). When Sjögren's syndrome dries up these glands, hoarseness can result, along with a feeling of constant congestion, of needing to clear the throat. A dry cough can develop, as well as frequent sore throats. The dryness here and in the mouth can, in severe cases, make speech difficult. Speaking for long periods, or singing, can put stress on a dry throat and vocal cords.

An irritation of the lining of the lungs (pleurisy or interstitial pneumonitis) makes the chest sore, but some researchers claim this occurs infrequently in SS, usually in combination with the diseases of secondary Sjögren's syndrome.[18] Bronchitis, shortness of breath,[19] and pneumonia are also possibilities, but there is controversy in the medical world as to how closely related these symptoms are to SS. [20,21,22,23,24] An example is the story of Kathy Marsh who moved south to Houston to avoid the hard winters that seemed to be making her ill, and later, suddenly and unexpectedly became desperately ill with pneumonia. Intensive care and a month's hospitalization pulled her through that but she had two recurrences. Even after her complaints about her dry mouth finally turned up a diagnosis of SS, her doctors disagree as to whether the pneumonia is a function of the Sjögren's. Constantopoulos says some recent studies have shown that pneumonia and respiratory infections are not more common in SS patients than others.[25] He concludes this may be because of newer ways of treating SS, especially a decrease in the use of immunosuppressives.

The patient with a dry cough may be treated for asthma, bronchitis, or even tuberculosis before she is diagnosed with SS. Actually the dry cough may be caused

[18]Stavros H. Constantopoulos, E. V. Tsianos, and H. M. Moutsopoulos Pulmonary and Gastrointestinal Manifestations of Sjögren's Syndrome Rheumatic Clinics of America: Sjögren's Syndrome, Vol18, Number 3 pp617-635

[19]S. Constantopoulos et al "Xerotrachea and Interstitial Lung Disease in Primary Sjögren's Syndrome" Respiration 1984; 46: 310-314

[20]M Alexander "Clinical Aspects of Sjögren's Syndrome" Southern Medical Journal July 1986; 79: 857-862

[21]F. Bariffi et al "Pulmonary Involvement in Sjögren's Syndrome" Respiration 1984; 46: 82-87

[22]S. Constantopoulos et al "Respiratory Manifestations in Primary Sjögren's Syndrome Ioannina Greece: University of Ioannina

[23]M. Papathanasiou et al "Reappraisal of Respiratory Abnormalities in Primary and Secondary Sjögren's Syndrome" Chest September 1986; 90: 370-374

[24]C. Strimlan "Pulmonary Involvement in Sjögren's Syndrome" Chest June 1986; 89: 901-901

[25]Constantopoulos et al Rheumatic Disease Clinics of North America : Sjögren's Syndrome p 619

by dryness of the mucous linings of the tubes from th. throat to the lungs (tracheobronchial tree), which was noted by Sjögren himself as a part of the syndrome. The condition has been called *bronchitis sicca* and *xerotrachea*. The dry cough may also be caused by irritation of the lungs.

Nasal Passages and Ears

Similarly, mucous membranes in the nasal passages may dry up, causing burning or itching (rhinitis). Irritations can lead to nosebleeds that seem to happen just to spite you. And, as in the eyes, compensatory efforts by the struggling glands can bring on the stuffiness of congestion. The same process that robs some patients of their tasting abilities is also at work here, interfering with the sense of smell.[26] The pathways (eustachian tubes) between the middle ear and the throat can be affected causing inflammation and a (generally) slight loss of hearing. Sara Endress reports, after years of eye and throat problems, that her ears are beginning to hurt, especially when in a draft from air conditioning. She finds putting cotton in them provides some protection. Sara lives in Arizona and uses a swamp cooler, a unit that adds moisture to the air it cools, instead of drying it as does an air conditioner. Now we are beginning to get an idea what is meant by "that ache all over feeling."

---

[26]Henkin et al Abnormalities of Taste and Smell in Sjögren's Syndrome, 375-383

Vaginal Dryness

Une of those problems many women are reluctant to discuss with their doctors is vaginal dryness. Or if they do complain to a gynecologist, they are often treated for recurring infections. Or if no infection is found, "vaginitis" is the diagnosis and we are told to ignore it and it will go away.

There are many causes of vaginal dryness. BioFilm, Inc., maker of the vaginal lubricant Astroglide, lists several, including menopause, breast feeding, birth control pills, hysterectomy, pregnancy, some medications, strenuous exercise and infections. Add to this the excess use of soap, douches, or bath powder. Even plain tap water can be the culprit. Soap, even mild soap, contains lye which is caustic. Prepared douches contain perfumes and dyes. Bath powder just naturally soaks up moisture. But tap water? Even the purest contains chemicals as well as traces of metal it picks up on its way through the plumbing pipes. The menstrual cycle, its ending, and changing hormone levels all have their effects. And, for once, it may actually be "all in your mind." Stress, fatigue, and an emotional upset can interfere with vaginal lubrication. Dryness can go along with "Not tonight, dear, I have a headache."

But for SS patients, it's the old story of glands that fail to function. There are two of them, called Bartholin's glands, located in the walls of the vagina, whose purpose is lubrication. As in other glands, lymphocytic infiltration can disrupt the ability to secrete the necessary fluids. And remember how our other beleaguered glands try hard to make up for the lack of their proper fluids? These are no exception, and the resulting mucous discharges mimic infections. Dryness and irritation invite frequent real infections, and it has been speculated that treatment for these can create a vicious cycle by causing more irritation. The lack of moisture can also bring pain to intercourse. Don't be too distressed by all this. Ways to prevent and/or alleviate these problems are discussed in the chapter on treatment.

Dry Skin

For some, a most annoying symptom is a dryness of the skin. The wrinkles that come with it make the skin look prematurely aged. Sjögren's syndrome patients also bruise easily. They may have rashes that hang around longer than ordinary hives would, small lumps (nodules) just under the skin, or sores and cracks. Purple marks (purpura) made by tiny broken and inflamed blood vessels (vasculitis) directly under the skin especially on the legs, may leave a brown coloring from iron deposits remaining after the bruise has faded. The surface of the skin may have small depressions from loss of fat under the skin, or nodules that appear as small lumpy spots under the skin.[27] Bernice Kapalin complains that at 55, this loss of fat cells has made her look "a lot older" than she is. SS patients do not sweat as easily, which may seem to the fastidious to be a plus, until one remembers that perspiration serves to cool and cleanse the skin. In fact, the lazy sweat glands actually cause the skin dryness. Another dimension added to the dry skin problem is a dry scalp and with it, dry hair.

---

[27]Michael Rozboril "The Impact of Sjögren's Syndrome on the skin" Sjögren's Digest National Sjögren's Syndrome Association Phoenix AZ 1993Vol.4,:1 pp3-4

While most of these skin problems are mere annoyances, it is important to note that the surface vasculitis, showing up as chronic hives or those purple marks on your legs, could be an indication of a more serious vasculitis going on in internal parts of your body. Though the cause is unknown, biopsies have shown infiltrations of neutrophils or lymphocytes (types of white blood cells) typical of SS. Vasculitis can impair the function of the gastrointestinal system, muscles, or the central nervous system (brain and spinal column). While this is relatively rare, the appearance of these outward markers should be a sign to investigate and eliminate the possibility of danger. This is an area where the condition is treatable and early diagnosis can help avoid trouble.

Extraglandular Symptoms

But hold on. There's more. Other complications vary considerably with each person. About one-fourth of the patients with primary Sjögren's syndrome have one or more of the following problems. Thus in our mythical Sicca City, with its 1000 Sjögren's syndrome patients, 250 fall into this category.

The blood vessels, spleen, liver, pancreas, muscles, and thyroid can all get into the act.[28] They, too, may become irritated and inflamed. About 150 of our Sicca City friends may have kidney problems. In addition, the digestive system and the central and peripheral nervous systems sometimes get involved.

Raynaud's phenomenon is a name given to the situation where the fingers become very sensitive to cold, heat, or emotional stress. They become white, then

---

28Talal, "How to Recognise and Treat Sjögren's Syndrome",80-87 blue, and may be numb or tingle and burn briefly before returning to normal.[29] At least one of my correspondents has complained that her feet are always cold.

The excessive need to urinate often comes as a side effect of the dry mouth that inspires a constant thirst and, consequently, continual drinking of fluids.

Under normal circumstances our kidneys are assigned the task of excreting wastes and regulating the body's water, electrolyte, and acid/base balance. This is accomplished, in part, by recycling the excess water we take in. In rare cases the marauding lymphocytes of Sjögren's syndrome inhibit that recycling ability. A short supply of antidiuretic hormones interferes with the kidneys' perception of water quantity. They simply excrete water, whether excess or not. As the body's water level goes down, the concentration of electrolytes goes up and the balance is disturbed. However, this happens extremely seldom and even then is usually so slight that you're not likely to notice it, so you should not be worried about it. Chances are, if you need to urinate often, it's because you are drinking a lot of fluids. This also results in a need to get up several times during the night. Irritation of the lining of the bladder (interstitial cystitis)[30] makes this problem worse when the bladder's walls swell and restrict its capacity. This is another one that often doesn't come to the attention of the rheumatologist. Your family doctor will refer you to a urologist who, quite naturally, will not be particularly concerned with the condition of your eyes and mouth.

---

[29]Arthritis Foundation, *Polymyositis and Dermatomyositis* Atlanta GA AF 1983
[30]E. Leonardo et al "Autoimmune Aspects in a Case of Chronic Interstitial Cystitis" *Minerva Medica* June 1986; 77

Digestive System

Acid-secreting glands in the stomach and mucous glands in the intestines become lazy and fail to do their jobs. Result? Poor digestion and unspecific pains that resist identification. Here there can be even more reason for confusion. By this time your doctor has surely prescribed some anti-inflammatory drugs, such as aspirin or ibuprofen. They are the subjects of the big TV commercial advertising campaigns based on the claims that they will not upset your stomach, but sometimes they do cause stomach problems for some people. They are even said to be responsible for the formation of ulcers, but how are we to know whether it is the pills or the illness that is causing the trouble?[31] According to Dr. Adolf Van Mulders and his associates, Sjögren's syndrome rather than the drugs may be the culprit.

The digestive process begins in the mouth when we chew our food. From that point on a series of mechanical and chemical steps break down the food for the body's use. Enzymes in the saliva initiate the action as the food passes quickly through the mouth and is carried down to the stomach. There, gastric glands secrete more enzymes, hydrochloric acid, and mucus, which combine to continue the process. Moving right along, the food (by now known as chyme) passes into the upper part of the intestine (the duodenum.) More glands secrete digestive juice from the pancreas to further convert the chyme. Digestion continues as the food elements are absorbed into the bloodstream and the residues are processed and moved out of the body.

---

[31] Adolf Van Mulders et al "Hypergastrinemia in Rheumatoid Arthritis Related to Sjögren's Syndrome" *The Journal of Rheumatology* 1984; 11: 246

From this brief account it is easy to see how anything that interferes with the action of all these glands can disrupt the whole digestive process. My correspondents complain variously of choking on dry food, of indigestion, abdominal pain, gas, constipation, diarrhea, nausea, diverticulitis, ulcers, frequent urination and bladder problems, although, admittedly, some of these may be only indirectly related to Sjögren's, if at all. We do have to use restraint in the tendency to blame *everything* on SS.[32]

From childhood I have had a digestive system that didn't follow the rules. For me, an apple a day did not keep the doctor away. In fact, apples and all those other high-fiber foods that are so popular now, aggravated the constipation that seemed always lurking, ready to plague me. It still does. And a high fiber, low-fat diet makes it worse. Only recently has it occurred to me to speculate about that relationship. Especially when I read that the way fiber helps is by absorbing moisture from the intestines, thus expanding and creating beneficial bulk. But we have learned that the SS patient is likely to have inefficient glands secreting insufficient digestive juices. Why wouldn't the thirsty fiber soak it all up and still be left too dry?

Dr. James Boyle of Case Western Reserve University School of Medicine describes some other problems that can be caused or complicated by SS.[33] Some patients have difficulty in swallowing (dysphagia). Although this has often been attributed to "webs" (the narrowing of the lowermost cartilage of the larynx), there can be a

---

[32]See pg for Survey information.
[33]James Boyle "The Digestive System and Sjögren's Syndrome," Synopsis of presentation at 3rd Annual NSSA Conference, Cleveland OH,19 Sept, '92 *Sjögren's Digest* Vol.4, Issue 1, 1993

variety of causes. The muscles of the esophagus may be weakened. They may not contract properly (dismotility), causing that swallowing problem as well as heartburn (acid rising from the stomach or refluxing), and chest pain that can frighten you into thinking you are having angina. Greek investigators Drs. Stavros H. Constantopoulos, Epaminondas V. Tsianos and Haralampos Moutsopoulos reviewed several studies and concluded that dismotility rather than webs or lack of saliva, is the main problem. That in turn could be caused by inflammation of the muscles (myositis) or of the glands in the esophagus.[34]

The most common digestive problem in SS may be gastritis, the plain old nagging tummy ache that comes from a lack of acid, rather than the familiar "excess acidity" the advertisers love to tout. In this case the pain, a burning sensation, and, for some people, nausea, is due to irritation of the stomach lining. Doctors call this shortage of digestive acids *achlorhydria.*

One component of saliva that may be in short supply for SS patients is epidermal growth factor. This helps control the growth of the stomach lining so that without it, the SS stomach walls may be thinner than normal and more susceptible to ulcers and erosion.

Chemicals called prostaglandins stimulate mucus and bicarbonate secretion in the stomach to help protect the lining. NSAIDs (non-steroidal anti-inflammatory drugs), often prescribed for arthritis, can reduce the production of prostaglandins, making already tender tissues easy victims for acids and other harmful chemicals.

---

[34]Constantopoulos et al *Rheumatic Disease Clinics of North America : Sjögren's Syndrome* p 627

We usually think of diabetes in connection with the pancreas, but for SS patients, inflammation of the pancreas is more likely. This is detected as an increase of the enzyme amylase in the blood, but there is a chance of confusion, since the excess amylase more often comes from the salivary glands. When it does come from the pancreas, it is usually harmless, causing no symptoms at all. A true pancreatitis is uncommon but more serious, with pain, fever, jaundice, and nausea that can be dangerous. Even more rare is a condition called adult celiac disease, or gluten enteropathy which is associated with malabsorption, a form of under-nutrition. In this case, the digested food is not properly absorbed through the mucous lining of the intestines into the bloodstream. Even with a good appetite, the patient doesn't get the full benefit from food.

Other serious situations can involve an inflammation of the liver (chronic active hepatitis), cirrhosis or inflammatory bowel disease.

These complications are relatively rare in proportion to the number of Sjögren's patients. Especially since the ones the gastroenterologist sees are only those who already have intestinal problems.

Central and Peripheral Nervous Systems

The relationship of the central nervous system (CNS) to SS is not universally accepted but some studies have shown that certain problems do occur. Included are mild memory lapses (who among us has not had an occasion to forget our best friend's name just when we need to introduce him to someone?), difficulties in concentration (and we thought that was just because the children were screaming at us!), and mild mood swings from excitement to depression. Some patients find they have less sensitivity to touch. Their fingers or toes may tingle, prickle, or just feel numb.[35] Some patients are afflicted with carpal tunnel syndrome, a tenderness and weakness of the thumb caused by pressure on a nerve at the wrist. Others report an inflammation of nerves in the arms, a "pinching feeling all over the body," random muscular jerks, and a loss of the sense of smell. Researchers are studying more serious manifestations they have observed in patients to learn whether these are related to SS or to other underlying conditions. The investigators are also unsure of the causes of these conditions in SS.[36]

Dr. Elaine Alexander considers central nervous system symptoms in SS patients to be "potentially treatable and reversible" in some cases.[37] Those with significant central nervous system problems may be helped by corticosteroids or immunosuppressive drugs. Because of the possibly serious side effects of these drugs, she recommends that patients be thoroughly checked before starting these treatments.

Lymphocytic Involvement

Sjögren's syndrome is a lymphoprolific condition; that is, the syndrome develops when the lymphocytes reproduce more freely than is normal in an undiseased state. Those excess white cells infiltrate the tear glands,

---

[35]H. Kaltreider et al "The Neuropathy of Sjögren's Syndrome" *Annals of Internal Medicine*, April 1969; 70: 751-761

[36]K. Malinow et al "Neuropsychiatric Dysfunction in Primary Sjögren's Syndrome" *Annals of Internal Medicine* 1985; 103: 344-349

[37]Elaine Alexander "Central nervous System Disease in Sjögren's Syndrome" *Rheum. Disaese Clinics of North America: Sjögren's Syndrome.* W. B. Saunders Co. Vol. 18:No. 3 August 1992 p637-672

the saliva glands, and other glands or organs, interfering with their functioning and thus causing the dryness that is the hallmark of Sjögren's. It has been shown that these events often follow one another in stages. A person may first notice a swollen saliva gland and only years later develop a problem with dry eyes, etc. Most of the time these invasions are considered "benign." Although the presence of the extra cells does cause some damage, the immediate results are generally not serious. Long-suffering victims may dispute having their problems being termed "not serious." I have always resented the television advertising that emphasizes the "minor aches of arthritis" when we all know that most of our aches are not minor at all! But all things are relative and in this case, serious means life-threatening. The symptoms of SS are inconvenient and uncomfortable but for the most part do not affect the lifespan of the patients. However certain troublesome problems can arise. In some patients the unbridled multiplication of the lymphocytes tends to form clusters which doctors refer to as *islands*. These groups of cells can give the appearance, in diagnostic tests, of tumors but may well not be malignant. In this case they are called *pseudo lymphomas*. They must be carefully watched since this imitation cancer may develop into a real malignancy, a true lymphoma. This is one of the reasons your doctor will monitor your blood serum components regularly. A drop in the level of immunoglobulin where there was previously a high count, and a decrease in RA factor can signal an alert for the approaching lymphoma state and let the doctor know action needs to be taken. While it has been estimated that fewer than 5% of primary SS patients may develop lymphoma,[38] as with all cancers, early diagnosis is extremely important. So your periodic blood checks take on added importance. The statistics indicating that lymphoma is rare are reassuring.

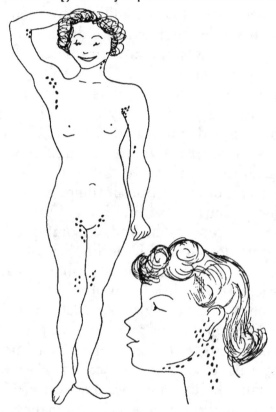

Figure 7 **Lymph Nodes for Self-Examination**

Dr. Talal does not want his patients to worry about that possibility. He tells them, "That's my job. I'm your doctor." He says, "I believe this. I don't take care of myself. I have a doctor. I let the doctor do the worrying for me."

By way of reassurance, he says there are now sophisticated technologies to detect and diagnose lymphomas. They can be picked up at the earliest appearance and there is effective treatment. The patient can help by noting any changes in her condition, such as swellings in the armpits or groin, or

[38]N. Pavlidis et al "The Clinical Picture of Primary Sjögren's Syndrome: a Retrospective Study" Journal of Rheumatology 1982; 9: 685-689

weight loss. He suggests a self examination similar to that done for breast cancer. Check the head and neck areas: behind the ears, down the neck muscle, and the armpits. An enlarged lymph node will be visible or palpable. You can see it, or if not, you can feel it. Why not examine your lymph node areas routinely along with the monthly breast exam? But Dr. Talal insists you should not make a fetish of it. "You don't worry constantly about getting hit by a car, and you shouldn't worry about lymphoma. Patients should have a doctor they have confidence in, who understands Sjögren's and he'll take care of it."

Allergies

Many Sjögren's patients are troubled with allergies, particularly stuffy noses and rashes. Although a direct relationship has not been established, this is another area where diagnosis can be confusing, since many of the symptoms of allergic disease can also be Sjögren's symptoms. Actually, an allergic reaction is an immune system response, but it involves a different mechanism. That makes it especially important to distinguish the cause of the problem so effective treatment can be carried out. If your stuffy nose really comes from your Sjögren's, treating it with antihistamines can do more harm than good.

An allergic reaction happens when three elements are present: IgE (immunoglobulin E), a protein that acts as an antibody, found in unusually high concentrations; white blood cells (mast cells) containing the chemical histamine; and an allergen, the substance to which you are allergic. This could be almost anything:

foods, feathers, the chemicals in detergents, pollens, even plain old mold or household dust. The way it all happens is that the IgE latches on to a histamine-loaded mast cell. When this potent combo sights the particles of pollen you have inhaled, which are now circulating around your nasal passages, it lets fly with a blast of histamine. This irritating stuff brings on the itching, sneezing, and congestion we all know so well. This is a delayed reaction, in that the first time you are exposed to a substance, you will not react but your immunoglobulins will be sensitized to it and remember. Sometime later, possibly the second time you are exposed, or possibly not till many years and many exposures later, the IgE/mast cell team will react unpleasantly when it recognizes that same allergen.

Of particular interest to the Sjögren's patient is the fact that these reactions could consist of a set of symptoms like a stuffed up head, post-nasal drip, congested ears, and swollen glands. Sound familiar? Right. All of these can also occur with SS, and we are back to the old problem of misdiagnosis. Maybe what you have treated as an allergy all these years is actually just one more aspect of your Sjögren's. But it is important to realize you can have both. One does not necessarily exclude the other; both possibilities must be explored to determine the proper treatment.

Fatigue

A quick reading of the past chapter leaves one with little surprise at the information that Sjögren's syndrome generally brings fatigue and over-all weakness! Patients say they frequently feel drained of energy and need to rest during the day. One can be tooling along tending to business as usual and suddenly just "crash." Some patients must carefully conserve their energy but, fortunately for most of us, a short rest will usually restore the lost vim, at least for the time being.

The previous paragraph was the complete section on fatigue in the "Sneaky" book, but on rereading the rest of the book, I find that I mentioned the word *fatigue* 23 times! Obviously, fatigue is a major factor in SS, and as such deserves much more attention. It can be a major disabling influence in our lives, but until fairly recently, fatigue has been considered more of a personality defect than a symptom. Lazy, goof-off, and couch potato are some of the terms used to describe the hapless victims. "You're fired." is another. When it finally began to be thought of as an illness, it was called "yuppie flu."

Now, however, more and more physicians and scientists are recognizing fatigue as either a disease entity (Chronic Fatigue Syndrome/CFS or Chronic Fatigue and Immune Dysfunction Syndrome/CFIDS) or a symptom in an associated disease, such as Sjögren's syndrome. The CFIDS Association of America has lobbied Congress to commit the NIH, the CDC, and Social Security Administration to recognize and aggressively research the disease. An international CFIDS Conference was held in Albany, NY in October of 1992, with researchers, physicians, and patients from 30 countries reporting on their work and expressing their concerns. Clearly, chronic fatigue is no longer considered a matter for a psychiatrist. Studies have indicated that the disease is likely to be multifactorial, as is SS, and several viruses have been looked at as contributing to the cause. Epstein-Barr Virus (EBV) and HHV-6 (a type of herpes virus) have been considered, but neither has been found in all patients. The search for a cause continues.

While CFIDS itself is not considered to be directly related to SS, Dr. Leonard Calabrese reported on a group of patients who had both CFIDS and Sjögren's syndrome.[39] It is interesting that, along with lupus, these diseases with major fatigue problems are immune system disorders. Any successful research into one of them is bound to be helpful to the others.

Meanwhile, fatigue is a large part of our daily lives and must be considered a primary symptom of SS. Dr. Robert S. Schwartz of Tufts University School of Medicine offers one explanation for the extreme fatigue that he describes as being like "swimming upstream against a strong tide." He writes [40], that the inflammatory response in an autoimmune disease causes the lymphocytes to send out signals. A lymphokine (peptide) called Interleukin-1 (IL-1) inspires certain brain cells to produce yet another peptide that causes sleep. Normally this serves a purpose. When you are sick, say with the flu, you are sleepy and perfectly willing to get the rest the body needs for the healing process. In our case, with the immune system working overtime and inflammation happening in many parts of our body, it's no wonder we feel exhausted.

Ways of dealing with fatigue are discussed in Section II of this book.

---

[39]Tom Hennessy "Light at the End of the Tunnel" *New York Native* Nov. 9 1992 p13

[40]Robert S. Schwartz "Fatigue and the Lupus Patient" *Lupus News* Vol. 9, No.2 1989 pp1-2

Neonatal Lupus

Pregnant women who have, or suspect they may have Sjögren's syndrome should be aware of the possibility of a lupus-like condition that can affect their baby. On exposure to sunlight, the baby may develop a rash much like that of a lupus patient. This is no cause for concern as it will go away of its own accord and does not need treatment. More serious is the heart blockage that can impair the infant's heart's ability to coordinate the beating of its valves, a possibly fatal defect. While some doctors have recommended abortion if a heart blockage is detected, current treatments can make that unnecessary. The heart blockage can now be overcome by the use of a pacemaker. While this only affects a small proportion of SS patients, all mothers whose blood tests positive for the SS-A/antiRo antibody should be checked early in their pregnancy to see if they have the particular type of antigens that will cause the problem. It is essential that they be carefully monitored with X rays and other techniques for managing high risk pregnancy. Be *sure* to tell your gynecologist (or any other doctor) about your Sjögren's syndrome! [41,42]

Secondary Sjögren's Syndrome

About 50 percent of all Sjögren's syndrome patients have the condition as a secondary manifestation of another connective tissue disease. It can be associated with rheumatoid arthritis, systemic lupus erythematosus,

---

[41]Norman Talal, HM Moutsopoulos, Stuart Kassan, eds *Sjögren's Syndrome, Clinical and Immunological Aspects* Berlin; Springer-Verlag: August 1987
[42]Elaine Alexander "The Relationship Between Anti-RO Positive Sjögren's Syndrome and Anti-RO Positive Lupus Erythematosus" 323-330

scleroderma, polymyositis, dermatomyositis or mixed connective tissue disease (MCTD). [43] Most frequently it coexists with RA and, in fact, it had been hard until lately to tell if a patient actually had RA or just primary Sjögren's syndrome with strong symptoms mimicking RA. However, the criteria for separating the two conditions have been pretty well established in recent years.

Rheumatoid Arthritis

Rheumatoid arthritis is a systemic disease, afflicting many parts of the body. Symptoms may range from the minor discomfort of aching joints to crippling deformities of severe forms of the disease. Like Sjögren's syndrome, it is an autoimmune disease, in which certain antibodies in the bloodstream turn against healthy cells instead of attacking invading disease cells. In RA the major targets are the joints. But it can also damage muscles, lungs, skin, blood vessels, nerves, and eyes. These common symptoms bring about some of the confusion with Sjögren's syndrome, but there are tests to measure the blood factors that positively identify RA. As many as 25% of all RA patients also have Sjögren's syndrome. [44]

Systemic Lupus Erythematosus

An even higher percentage (up to 30%) of patients with lupus have Sjögren's syndrome, but, according to University of Texas Health Science Center im-

---

[43]Donato Alarcon-Segovia "Symptomatic Sjögren's Syndrome in Mixed Connective Tissue Disease" *The Journal of Rheumatology;* 1984; 11: 582-583
[44]Arthritis Foundation *Rheumatoid Arthritis* Atlanta GA: AF; 1983

munologist Dr. Frank Arnett, distinguishing primary Sjögren's syndrome with lupus-like symptoms from Sjögren's syndrome secondary to lupus can still be a problem, even for the experts. When you consider that joint pain in hands, wrists, elbows, knees, or ankles; skin rashes; fatigue and weakness; and swollen glands are all early symptoms of lupus, you realize how a patient complaining of those things could be thought to have lupus when she may possibly have primary Sjögren's syndrome instead. Lupus, like Sjögren's syndrome, is a chronic, systemic, inflammatory auto-immune disease. Dr. Elaine Alexander, working at Johns Hopkins University, suggests that the close relationship of the two conditions may be the result of similar immunogenetic backgrounds of the patients. [45]

As in Sjögren's syndrome, there are no cures for lupus, only ways to treat or to stave off problems. The lupus patient's skin will likely be extra sensitive to sunlight, and she may experience a lack of appetite and muscle aches. Kidneys can be affected, and the linings of the heart and lungs could be attacked. The fact that depression often comes as a part of the illness is not surprising[46]

Scleroderma

Four to five percent of all Sjögren's patients have associated scleroderma, a chronic, systemic, connective tissue disease. Once more the similarity is noted in the effects of the disease on the skin, joints, kidneys, blood vessels, digestive system, and lungs. The muscles may

[45]Alexander "The Relationship Between Anti-RO Positive Sjögren's Syndrome and Anti-RO Positive Lupus Erythematosus" 323-330

[46]Arthritis Foundation *Systemic Lupus Erythematosus* Atlanta GA: AF; 1984

also be attacked. Raynaud's phenomenon (fingers sensitive to cold) is an early symptom of scleroderma. Holding an icy cold drink glass in your hand, or getting angry triggers a narrowing of the small blood vessels of the fingertips causing the fingers to change color, first to white and then blue, and tingle or turn numb. Problems specific to scleroderma include swelling of the fingers or toes and a hardening of the skin from which the condition derives its name. "Sclero" comes from a Greek word meaning hardening; "derma" refers to skin. Various internal organs and systems can be affected by this thickening process with an accompanying loss of function.[47]

Polymyositis and Dermatomyositis

In the myositis illnesses, the immune system aims for the muscles, generating heat, redness, pain, and loss of function in those targets. Since muscles provide the support for our bony framework, weakness is the end result of the inflammation of the muscles. In dermatomyositis, skin rashes are evident along with the weakness. The patient may develop purplish-red patches around the eyes, as Betty Rosen did. Patients may have further symptoms such as fever, Raynaud's phenomenon, or, rarely, tumors. Polymyositis and dermatomyositis are the least common of the diseases we are discussing, with no more than 5 out of a million Americans being diagnosed each year.[48]

The diagnosis of muscle disease is sometimes confused with fibromyalgia (or fibrositis.) This is an

---

[47]Arthritis Foundation *Scleroderma* Atlanta GA: AF; 1983
[48]Arthritis Foundation, *Polymyositis and Dermatomyositis*

arthritis-related condition causing muscle and tendon pain at specific points of the body. Though it is too frequently given the "all-in-the-mind" treatment, diagnosis can be established by pressure at the series of "trigger points." Other symptoms can include chest pain, concentration difficulty, painful menstruation, headaches, frequent and/or painful urination, diarrhea/constipation, numbness in arms or legs, depression, Reynaud's phenomenon, dryness, tendonitis, and/or dizziness.

Not known to be related to SS, it nevertheless seems to occur often in SS patients. Treatment involves heat and/or cold, aerobic exercise, correct posture, some pain relieving drugs, and stress management. Research is growing and there is an association to provide support (see Appendix I: Support Resources).

Conclusion

It's obvious by now that the symptoms of SS are far-reaching and varied. Actually there are even more possible combinations of symptoms, but they occur so rarely that it hardly seems worth adding them to an already too long list. Fortunately, no one patient is dealt a full hand of all these ills. In fact, that very difference from patient to patient adds to the complexity of the illness and produces an astonishingly diverse population of SS victims. Remember there are many things doctor and patient can do to alleviate most of the listed symptoms, and even to prevent the more serious consequences of SS.

Chapter 3 - Immunology

What's Happening?

Our bodies are astonishingly complex machines. You have only to consider the structural design of the eye to be convinced of that. The old joke, "God must have known we'd eventually need to wear glasses; otherwise why would he put the ears where he did?" expresses my sense of wonder at the orderliness of our construction and the processes by which we operate.

The immune system is probably the most fascinating of all the departmentalized functions of the body. Even the most simplified description of the processes involved in protecting us from the forces bent on our destruction reads like a chronicle of global wars. A virtual army of white blood cells stands ready, at the first hint of foreign invasion, to mobilize itself against the threat. The troops consist of soldiers with names like phagocytes and lymphocytes, each with specific duties and skills to wage the battles. What's more, the various cells have a language by which they communicate strategies and the means to identify their enemies.

Only recently have scientists been able to begin to unravel the mysteries of how these things can be. Electron microscopes and revolutionary new technologies have allowed them to see and study and manipulate organisms so small the average person cannot even envision them. Tiny cells can now be magnified as much as 500,000 times and forced to reveal their secrets. So, though there are still many holes in the data, and new questions are constantly being raised, the researchers are beginning to be able to piece together the amazing conflict that is constantly carried on within our bodies.

White Cell Warriors

Whenever an enemy agent, whether virus, bacteria, or protozoa, attacks us, it enters the body and seeks out the host cell it needs to reproduce and function. A virus, for instance, is not self-sufficient. It has only the instruction manual to carry out its work, not the necessary materials. For these it must locate and commandeer a particular type of cell. Using a specialized identification system, it locates the proper host, invades it and uses the cell's facilities to reproduce itself. These new viruses, in turn, break out of the cell to find new ones of their own to occupy, taking them over and repeating the process, creating many new viruses at each step. But all the while certain white blood cells that originate in the bone marrow, called phagocytes, have been cruising the body's blood vessel highways, keeping an eye out for trouble. When they spot it, they go into action quickly. Swift and efficient killers, they engulf the invading viruses and devour them. But the viruses can multiply faster than the phagocytes can consume them, so help is available from another group of white blood cells, the lymphocytes, or T cells. There are three types of T cells: the helpers, the killers and the suppressors. The first, the helpers, circulate constantly throughout the bloodstream, keeping the system under surveillance, like a scouting task force. When T cells programmed to recognize our particular unfriendly virus, spot the trouble the phagocytes are having, they come to the rescue. First they send out a call for reinforcements that brings more phagocytes and T cells to join the battle. But then they also go racing off to the nearest lymph node, where the back up troops, the killer T cells, are just waiting to be alerted. Stimulated by the helper cells, the killers hurriedly reproduce themselves, increasing their number substantially. These newly created soldiers then rush to the battle field. There they help out by killing off the infected host cells before the viruses can reproduce in them.

Meanwhile, back at the lymph node, the helper T cells have another job to do. They must also stir up yet another group of lymphocytes, the B cells. On orders from the helper cells, the B cells, like their T cell brothers before them, start to reproduce themselves. But at the same time, they begin to manufacture chemical weapons called antibodies (or immunoglobulins). The antibodies, specifically designed to attack the particular virus that's causing all the fuss, join the others at the battlefield and begin the work of destroying the viruses themselves, before the viruses can enter the host cells and begin to reproduce. Together with the phagocytes and killer T cells which have been holding the fort waiting for the slower B cells to do their work, the antibodies make short work of finishing off the invaders. From somewhere (no one is quite sure where) a contingent of "marines", non T cell types known as natural killer (NK) cells with the power to attack a variety of enemies, also joins the fray. [49] When the war

[49] Y Ichikawa et al "Circulating Natural Killer Cells in Sjögren's syndrome" *Arthritis and Rheumatism* Feb 1985; 28: 182-187

is finally won, a new type of T cell, a suppressor cell, comes on the scene to sound the all clear, telling the killer cells and the B cells to take off for some R & R leave. The scavenging phagocytes, who, like goats, will eat anything, clean up the mess and the remaining T and B cells hang around, as memory cells, to make darn sure those bad guys don't come back. Or if they do, we're on the ready. It is this last feature that accounts for the immunity that develops after a person has once experienced a particular kind of disease, such as mumps.

Humoral Immunity

Two distinct types of action are going on in the warfare just described. The phagocytes, T cells, and B cells are engaged in a mechanical process using direct attacks on the cells to do their work. This is referred to as *cellular immunity*, while the action of the antibodies is chemical, and since it takes place in the serum (a *humor*, or functioning fluid) is known as *humoral immunity*. The antibodies are proteins specifically designed to combine with a certain antigen, the protein that identifies the invading virus. In doing so they serve several functions. They can hold down the virus so the phagocyte can more easily surround it; they can keep the virus from attaching to a host cell; or they can neutralize toxins put out by bacteria. Beyond this, these versatile warriors can simply burst the enemy cell. There are many different kinds of antibodies which, in addition to targeting different enemy cells, belong to five separate classes programmed to serve different functions. Of particular interest to Sjögren's patients are those known as IgA. Secreted on mucous membranes they are capable of neutralizing viruses before they actually enter the body. One of the techniques of diagnosing Sjögren's involves the observation of excess concentrations of IgA in the saliva.

System Breakdowns

Immune system diseases, and particularly autoimmune disorders, are those that occur when some part of this elaborate protective system fails to function properly. From its very nature, you can see how there are many opportunities for malfunctions at various stages of the process. In some cases the invading virus can turn off the immune system, stopping the phagocytes and killer cells in their tracks. Sometimes the defenders become weakened by dietary lacks on the part of the host. Malnutrition cripples the thymus gland, the body's T cell producing factory. Some medications, particularly cancer chemotherapy can effectively suppress the immune system. In fact these same drugs are the ones used for that purpose in fighting the rejection of transplanted organs. Severe burns can seriously reduce the responsiveness of the immune system. But there is also a range of congenital defects that can result in immune deficiencies. And it is in this area that researchers think lies the basis for Sjögren's syndrome, as well as the other autoimmune diseases.

Autoimmunity

Probably the most amazing and puzzling aspect of the immune system is the ability of killer T cells and antibodies to recognize other cells, and to distinguish friend from foe. Each cell, and each invading entity (antigen) wears a badge, a genetic label constructed of proteins which, like a combination lock, is specific for one type of virus, hepatitis, for instance, and that one only. A killer cell programmed to intercept a hepatitis virus will completely ignore any other virus it bumps into on its journey, but immediately mobilize against any hepatitis virus it meets. The ability to know when NOT to react violently to another substance is called *immune tolerance*, and it is the breakdown of immune tolerance that allows a confused T cell to attack the healthy tissues of its host.

A Trouble-Making Trio

Researchers do not yet know what causes these self-destructive attacks to occur, but they have recently concluded that, far from being a rare aberration that mysteriously appears in the bloodstream, the self destructive cells are there right along, but, in the normal bloodstream, are being prevented from acting. Some studies show that helper T cells somehow gain the upper hand over the suppressor T cells whose job it is to keep them in check. It is the breakdown of these controls that is now thought to trigger the destructive course of RA, lupus, and the other autoimmune diseases, including Sjögren's syndrome. Still to be discovered are the factors that bring about the release of the dormant cells. Evidence points to a slow-growing virus, one that can hide, somehow, from the killer cells and live in the body many years in a cocoon-like state. Some event, a trauma or stressful situation, could activate the virus and stimulate the T cells. So it becomes a possibility that the cause of Sjögren's may be made up of four elements: an inherited genetic pre-disposition (self-destructive killer cells as part of the equipment some people are born with), a virus that gains entry early in life and lies in waiting, a possible hormonal involvement, and an event that stirs all of them to action.

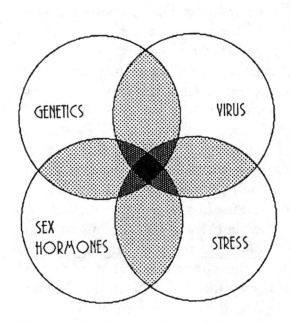

Figure 8 **Factors in Autoimmunity**
(Adapted from diagram by
Dr. Norman Talal)

A person could have the genetic tendency to acquire an immune system disease, but never encounter the virus that would activate it. Or on the other hand, the virus would be rendered harmless if the mixed-up T cells were not present or were never awakened. Under this theory, it would take the combination of all four circumstances to create a case of Sjögren's syndrome. [50]

Sexual Innuendoes

An important fourth element in the equation suggests itself in the fact that Sjögren's syndrome, and

---

[50]S. Mizel, P Jaret *In Self Defense* New York Harcourt Brace Jovanovich, Publishers; 1985

most autoimmune diseases, strike women much more often than men. Although this little piece of natural chauvinism had long been noted, it was not until 1972 that a report by the Arthritis Foundation-sponsored National Advisory Committee on the Future of Arthritis Research urged that an explanation be sought. Since that time, studies have been initiated at the immunology laboratories at the University of Texas Health Science Center in San Antonio under Dr. Norman Talal and Dr. S. Ansar Ahmed.[51] Researchers there are exploring the possibility that this difference is moderated by sex hormones. Evidence shows that women have heightened immune systems, which may strengthen their defenses against infections and tumors. This could explain their greater longevity and also help in reproduction, thus protecting the survival of the species. But at the same time this may be what makes them more susceptible to autoimmune diseases. On the other side of the coin, men with certain autoimmune diseases seem to have lower levels of male sex hormones. The ongoing studies are working to uncover exactly how the hormones act on the lymphocytes.[52]

Translating Causes to Effects

We have seen the sometimes devastating effects of the lack of moisture and discussed the possible reasons for the shortages but at times its hard to connect cause and effect. Why, for instance, would a simple loss of water in the mouth have all those repercussions? The an-

---

[51]Norman Talal Curiculum Vitae May 8, 1987

[52]*Rheumatology/Clinical Immunology Fellowship Training*, Dept. of Medicine, UT Health Science Center at San Antonio; 1987

swer lies in the fact that saliva is not simply water. Far from it. It is a complex solution of ingredients with specific functions that are sorely missed by the SS patient. Though predominantly water, saliva is also swimming with blood cells, immunoglobulins, enzyme-containing proteins, and lactoferrin, all carefully pH balanced.[53,54] All these components work together in the normal mouth to keep the natural balance in force. Antibodies gather together excess bacteria to be eliminated from the mouth. Enzymes deactivate them. Amino acids help control bacteria and fungus. Chloride thiocyanate, calcium, phosphate, and bicarbonate maintain the proper level of acidity and alkalinity while the calcium and phosphates in the saliva stand ready to replenish any lack of those minerals on the teeth. Lactoferrin (a natural saliva component) in normal amounts helps protect the mouth from bacterial infections, but in the increased quantities found in SS, upsets the normal migration patterns of the T cells, attracting them like a magnet to the affected glands, and actually contributing to the tissue destruction.[55] Another one of those important ingredients of saliva is intrinsic factor, essential for utilizing vitamin B-12.

I'll bet you won't ever again think of saliva as just mouth water! The saliva glands bring to mind a chocolate factory in which various ingredients are poured from assorted tubes into enormous vats and constantly blended to make just the right mix. Hold back some of the sugar and the gooey stuff is too bitter. Too much of

---

[53]James Sciubba et al Moderator "Report on September '86 Symposium: Living with Sjögren's Syndrome, Part 2." *Moisture Seekers Newsletter* Great Neck NY; June 1987; 4: 6, 1-5

[54]Konttinen, T. Yrio et al "Lactoferrin in Sjögren's Syndrome" *Arthritis and Rheumatism*; April 1984; 27: 462-466

[55]Katz *G-I Problems*

another ingredient and it might not be the right consistency. In saliva the composition is regulated by the glands' activity. The flow rate changes as needed and is influenced by many factors such as your diet. Sweet treats stimulate it and certain foods (persimmons, for instance) can dry it up in a hurry. Thus the famous pucker. But it is not just the amount but the actual proportion of ingredients that changes. Not only that, but the glands can get tired from all that busywork. After that great Christmas dinner, they definitely need a rest and time to refill their tanks. SS patients learn to be extremely careful what they put in their mouths, and when.

Why Me?

It is almost impossible not to wonder, specifically, where do I come in? How did I get involved in all this? And should my children be worried about getting it? What about their children? When a young prospective parent asks me that question, my best answer is that none of my problems has yet made me wish I hadn't been born. But it is of legitimate concern to patients and their families. And to the doctors trying to solve the puzzles.

In most cases, a person who has Sjögren's syndrome has never heard of it before diagnosis. No one she knows and no one in her family has it. Studies have been done to determine if Sjögren's syndrome is inherited, and indicate that certain genetic factors show up in the blood of the majority of patients. These factors have been identified as anti-Ro (SS-A) and anti-La (SS-B) antibodies,, and HLA-DR3, DR4, DR2, DRw52, and other histocompatibility antigens.

Lysozyme	Destroys, inhibits bacteria.
Lactoferrin	Deprives certain bacteria of essential ferric iron. Destroys major tooth decay bacteria.
Lactoperoxidase	Helps disrupt bacterial enzymes.
Histidine-rich proteins (HRPs)	Inhibits fungus (Candida albans).
Antibodies	Against polio virus and cold virus.
Mucins	Anti-viral Coat and lubricate oral tissues. Protect against toxins and irritants in foods possibly including carcinogens such as tobacco smoke.
	Coat food, easing passage through digestive system. Coat, protect teeth, - keeps acid from out of teeth and minerals in.
Calcium phosphate salts and other minerals	Build tooth enamel, repair early cavities.
Statherin	Keep salts in solution in saliva.
Proline-rich proteins	Remineralization Lubricants Possible anti-carcinogenic effect by binding tannin-rich foods which may cause esophageal cancer.
Phosphoproteins (cystatins)	Prevent oral tissue destruction by plaque and degenerating white cells.
Epidermal Growth Factor	Helps heal wounds and repair epidermal tissue (in animals. Effects not known in humans.)

Figure 9 **Some Components of Saliva and Their Actions[56]**

---

[56] Oral Soft Tissues, Salivary Glands and Saliva, and AIDS" *Broadening the Scope*National Institutes of Health

Immunologists are still studying the patterns of occurrence of these factors and their implications for the likelihood of a particular person getting Sjögren's syndrome. More, they are hopeful that this information will help predict the probable course of the disease. Thus, if it is found that a patient has a certain component of genes, this person will be more or less likely to have serious complications, which in turn, can then be anticipated and treated as required.

Also, some components have been found to cross the boundaries of the various diseases. Part of the difficulty in diagnosing SS lies in the fact that it shares some blood factors with rheumatoid arthritis, and even more so with lupus. Seeing an indicator of lupus (or RA) in the blood chemistry can lead to a confused impression that lupus (or RA) is present.

In studies of families, a cluster of different autoimmune diseases is more often found than a grouping of several members with the same disease. An SS patient's sister may have RA, while a cousin has scleroderma, but it is rare for several members of the same family all to have SS. The author's mother had a swollen parotid gland removed as a child (that was around the turn of the century and she lived to be 96 years old, well and chipper with no sign of autoimmune illness!). Her brother had multiple sclerosis (thought to have an autoimmune origin),[57] and an aunt had a thyroid disease (goiter). Since it has also been shown that affected family members do not necessarily share the same HLA complexes,[58] it is believed that a com-

[57]Elaine Alexander "Primary Sjögren's Syndrome with Central Nervous System Disease Mimicking Multiple Sclerosis" *Annals of Internal Medicine:* 1986; 104: 323-330

[58]John D. Reville et al "Primary Sjögren's Syndrome and Other Autoimmune Diseases in Families" Annals of Internal Medicine; 194; 101: 748-756

bination of genetic effects (hereditary predisposition) and environmental triggers influence the disease statistics. Identifying these elements may even lead eventually to ways to prevent the development of immune disorders.[59] Important to this hope is the ability to distinguish between primary and secondary SS. As we have stated, Sjögren's syndrome is considered primary when it occurs without any other well-defined rheumatic disease. When the rheumatic disease is present, the Sjögren's is considered secondary. The patient suffering from acutely dry eyes and mouth may not be much concerned at the moment with being put in a particular pigeonhole. Both sets of victims are likely to have these problems, and aching joints, too. After all, that is the definition we have already set up. Two out of three symptoms lets you into the not so exclusive club of Sjögren's syndrome. But there are significant differences. Obviously, its a relief if you hear, as I did, "there's no way you could have had RA for twenty years and show no sign of it in the joints of your hands." Those words lifted the sentence I had been under for all those years: the specter of an old age marred by crippling deformities and possibly spent in a wheelchair. On the other side of the coin, if you do have RA, the effects of the Sjögren's are likely to be less disturbing. But more importantly, the distinctions still being revealed by ongoing research will make the management of the condition much more accurate. Studies indicate that instead of a catchall situation, we are dealing with two distinct entities. The differences are clearly indicated not only in clinical mani-

[59]Frank C. Arnett "HLA Genes and Predisposition to Rheumatic Diseases" *Hospital Practice* 1986: 89-100

festations but also in the serologic and genetic markers. Where the circulating antibodies mentioned earlier are positive signs of Sjögren's syndrome, some are predominantly present in PSS and absent in RA-SS and some just the opposite. Primary SS patients may carry the RA factor and antinuclear antibodies (indicative of lupus)-without having those diseases. The presence of SS-A (in PSS) seems to indicate a greater possibility of complications such as vasculitis. Antibodies against salivary ducts appear much more frequently in secondary SS. The antigens HLA-B8[60] and HLA-DR3 are associated most often with primary SS, while HLA-Dw52 (MT2)[61] is found in both.

Symptoms that help differentiate include more frequent swelling of the face, jaws, or neck; and more of a need to make those night time trips to the bathroom. Thyroid involvement, showing up as sluggishness, is most often seen in primary SS. The primary form also more commonly includes the smarting fingers (Raynaud's phenomenon), the burgundy colored skin splotches (purpura), and muscle weakness (myositis).[62] The joint pains of primary SS are generally milder than those of RA and most often affect the smaller joints, without, as we have noted, bringing on the deformity of those joints.

---

[60]Haralampos M. Moutsopoulos et al "Differences in the Clinical Manifestations of Sicca Syndrome in the Presence and Absence of Rheumatoid Arthritis" *The American Journal of Medicine* May 1979; 66:733-736

[61]Douglas A. Jabs et al "Familial Abnormalities of Lymphocyte Function in a Large Sjögren's Syndrome kindred" The Journal of Rheumatology 1986; 13: 320-326

[62]April Bogle Booth "Walking for Arthritis" *Arthritis Today,* October 1987: 10-12

Chapter 4 - History

The story of our knowledge of Sjögren's syndrome is one of many doctors picking up on the different symptoms in different patients and gradually piecing together the picture of the systemic disease described in this book.

Filamentary Keratitis

The story begins on a particular day in 1882, when the Eye Clinic at Heidelberg Congress was holding an afternoon session.[63] Dr. Theodor Leber reported on three patients who particularly interested him. In each of the three, he had noticed strands or filaments attached to the corneas of the eyes. The strands were removed, but grew back. Leber called the condition filamentary keratitis. The next year Dr. Uhtoff showed drawings he had made of similar filaments which some viewers declared to look like coiled snakes or perhaps a garden hose.

Swollen Glands

When 42-year-old Christof Kalweit left his farm near Vienna to seek the help of the young doctor Johann von Mikulicz-Radecki, he was worried about

---

[63]Shearn *Sjögren's Syndrome*

puffy swellings around his eyes that were interfering with his sight. The enlarged tear glands were later echoed by swollen saliva glands. Mikulicz, surgical assistant to famed surgeon Dr. Christian Albert Theodore Billroth, removed the tumors but they reappeared two months later. There was a second operation and by the time Kalweit died of appendicitis several months later, the swellings were almost gone. Wishing to honor his mentor, Dr. Billroth, Mikulicz gave a paper describing the case before a symposium of the Society for Scientific Medicine at Konigsberg honoring the professor's academic achievements. And again in 1892, as a professor himself at Breslau, he published an account of Kalweit's history, noting that the condition was mild but with a tendency to relapse. Unfortunately, Mikulicz's work led to a confusing lumping of a variety of salivary gland conditions under his name, in spite of the fact that the doctor had clearly detailed the atrophy brought on by cell infiltrations of the glands in his patients. There was much confusion among medical circles as doctors rushed to get on the bandwagon, describing every case of swollen glands they saw as Mikulicz's disease. In 1907, a Dr. Napp proclaimed it to be merely a collection of symptoms that could be brought on by any number of other causes. By 1914, Dr. Thursfield had divided the syndrome into eight separate categories which were regrouped in 1927 back down to two groups classified as Mikulicz's disease resulting from known causes, or Mikulicz's disease resulting from unknown causes.

Xerostomia

In the meantime the association of dry eyes and a dry mouth, which he christened "xerostomia," was reported by Dr. Walter Baugh Hadden in 1888, but it took Dr. Fuchs, writing in 1919, to make the connection between tear gland deficiency and dry eyes as well as the association of swollen salivary glands and dryness of the mouth.

Gougerot's Syndrome

In the early twenties, the French physician, Dr. H. Gougerot, at the Hôpital San Louis in Paris, maintained that a general condition existed in which the eyes, mouth, larnyx, nose, and vulva all suffered from a related dryness which also affected the thyroid and ovaries. In fact, the syndrome is still referred to in France as "Gougerot's syndrome."

Arthritis

An elderly patient crippled with arthritis and at the same time suffering from the same filamentary cornea disease (keratitis) attracted the attention of Mulock Houwer in 1927. He began noticing that other patients had the same combination of symptoms, adding the third element of the syndrome, a finding confirmed by other studies and other physicians.

Sjögren's Keratoconjunctivitis

Swedish ophthalmologist Henrik Sjögren, fascinated by his first case of dry eyes, began a careful study of the condition in 1930. Born in October, 1899, in the Swedish town of Koping, young Henrik completed his medical studies at Stockholm's Karolinska Institute in 1927. He met Maria Hellgren, the daughter of a prominent ophthalmologist, composed a delightful waltz to honor their engagement, and married her while still in training for his own ophthalmology specialty at Serafimerlasarettet in Stockholm. During that time Sjögren saw a particular patient who piqued his interest. At 49, the woman had no tears for crying and couldn't swallow her food without a drink to wash it down. She had come in complaining of the "rheumatismus chronicus" that had bothered her for six years and the burning, itching sensation of a foreign body in her eyes. Intrigued, he checked her eyes with rose bengal staining and observed dry spots on her corneas.

After seeing four other similar cases the same year, Sjögren wrote them up for the Swedish Medical Association journal *Hygiea*. In that comprehensive report published in 1933, he dubbed the condition "keratoconjunctivitis sicca." He concluded that keratoconjunctivitis was only part of a larger complex of symptoms which involved the tear glands, the saliva glands, the mucous glands of the nasal passages, and swollen jaws. He noted the frequency of arthritis as an additional symptom.

Unfortunately for Sjögren, his thesis *Zur Kenntnis der Keratoconjunctivitis Sicca*, was not as highly praised then as it is now, and he was denied the necessary rank as Docent. As a result, he didn't pursue an academic career. Instead, he joined the staff of a hospital in southern Sweden where he continued his research. Sjögren was responsible for the adoption of the Schirmer test and rose bengal staining as diagnostic tools (See Chapter 5, Diagnosis and Testing). Sjögren's 20 years of work in identifying and recording the parameters of the disease was first honored with his name in 1936 when Von Grosz applied the name "Sjögren's syndrome" to the sicca complex. By the early forties his name was firmly attached to the syndrome he described and his once unappreciated thesis was translated into English and widely circulated.

Figure 10 Sabbatsberg Hospital's Eye Clinic (Henrik Sjögren in inset)

He continued publishing papers and giving talks on SS, making his way around the world and receiving many honors from the medical world. In 1957 he was finally awarded the title of Docent from the University of Gothenburg. He has been named to honorary membership in the American Rheumatism Association, the Swedish Rheumatology Society, and the Royal College of Physicians and Surgeons of Glasgow. [64] At the time the first Sjögren's syndrome symposium was held in Copenhagen, he was living at the Ribbingska home in Lund, Sweden, still alert and keeping up with scientific literature. Death claimed him on the 17th of September, 1986. [65]

Sjögren's vs. Mikulicz's

Other researchers followed, discovering the frequent association of Sjögren's syndrome with rheumatoid arthritis. Dr. S. Holm noted the similarities, but it was not until 1953 that the team of Dr. Winfield Morgan and Dr. Benjamin Castleman, presented a paper[66] before the Boston gathering of the New England Pathological Society in 1950 and the Fiftieth Annual meeting of the American Association of Pathologists and Bacteriologists in St. Louis in 1953, concluding that Sjögren and Mikulicz were actually describing the same disease. Sjögren himself had written that they should be thought of separately, even publishing a table to illustrate his reasoning. Morgan and Castleman started out studying Mikulicz's disease to discover what made the parotid gland act as it did in that syndrome.

[64]Frank A. Wollheim "Henrik Sjögren and Sjögren's Syndrome" *Scandinavian Journal of Rheumatology* 1986; Suppl: 61: 12-15

[65]Rolf Manthorpe, Jan Ulrik Prause "Message of Welcome" *Scandinavian Journal of Rheumatology* 1986; Suppl: 61: 11

[66]Winfield Morgan, Benjamin Castleman "A Clinicopathologic Study of 'Mikulicz's Disease'" *American Journal of Pathology* 1953; 29: p471

They recorded the findings that showed the lymphocytes' replacement of the gland's secreting cells, the multiplication of mucus-secreting cells and the clumping of connective tissue cells.[67] Later, while reviewing the cases of that study, Morgan found a significant number of cases where the patients had the three parts of Sjögren's syndrome: the dry eyes, the dry mouth, and the arthritis. Not only that, but an analysis of one his Sjögren's patients revealed changes just like the ones Morgan and Castleman had described, and in fact they were just as Mikulicz had seen them, sixty-five years earlier. The two syndromes were actually one. Even in those days the confusion came about because no two patients were exactly alike. As Shearn wrote in 1971:

> Those patients with dry eyes saw an ophthalmologist, whereas those with salivary gland involvement were seen by a surgeon or otolaryngologist. In a similar fashion, the internist and rheumatologist studying the articular manifestations of a patient might be totally unaware of the seemingly unimportant complaints of dry eyes or recurring parotitis.

Ongoing Research

In the years since Morgan and Castleman's original study, much has been done to further refine the criteria for diagnosis of Sjögren's. The American Rheumatism Association standards demonstrated the "intimate relationship" of Sjögren's syndrome with rheumatoid arthritis, scleroderma, polymyositis, polyarteritis,

---

[67]Shearn *Sjögren's Syndrome*

systemic lupus erythematosus, purpura hyperglobulinemia (a blood condition), and Hashimoto's thyroiditis (an inflammation of the thyroid gland). Dr. Hashimoto himself recognized the similar changes of the thyroid glands he studied and the salivary glands Mikulicz reported on. Continuing studies expand our knowledge of the diversity of Sjögren's syndrome. Later we'll explore the work of researchers around the world that is ongoing in the 90s. The studies not only deal with the ramifications of the disease but also look into the probable hereditary and triggering factors that bring about the changes of Sjögren's syndrome.

Chapter 5 - Diagnosis and Testing

All right, if you've read this far, you surely have dry eyes and aches and pains all over your body. It could be what's known as *medical student's disease,* the power of suggestion. Every student in every medical school suffers from all the symptoms he studies about. But if you've had some of the symptoms you've read about here for a long time, it's probably making you wonder. How can the average person know if those symptoms mean he (or she) has Sjögren's syndrome? It's worth mentioning them to your doctor. He or she can investigate the possible causes. For every symptom that can be part of SS, there are assorted other possible causes. Dry eyes can be the result of chemicals in the air, dust irritation, or certain medications. Drugs can also dry up your mouth and throat, as can cigarette smoking or chemotherapy. We all know many things can make the joints ache. The biggest villain of all can be simple stress. The deadline you have to meet at the office or the husband who drives you up the wall can put a crick in your neck faster than a chilling draft. A rugged tennis game can wreck your elbows and Grandma insists it's the rain comin' tomorrow that does it. But if those problems go away and the aches don't, its time to see your doctor and tell all. He can use many tests and diagnostic procedures to pin down the source of the trouble.

Diagnostic Criteria

The Copenhagen Symposium and the Four Criteria

One of the most frustrating things about SS is the problem of diagnosis. Three or four medical organizations have set up criteria for establishing a clinical diagnosis of SS, but none agree totally. In September, 1986, the First International Symposium on Sjögren's Syndrome was held in Copenhagen, Denmark under the leadership of Dr. Jan Ulrik Prause of the University of Copenhagen Institute of Eye Pathology, and Dr. Rolf Manthorpe of Sweden's University of Lund. Papers were presented by doctors from the US, Denmark, Sweden, Canada, England, Greece, Japan, and other countries.

One of the main items of business was to establish an international set of criteria for the diagnosis of Sjögren's syndrome. This is extremely important, not only for the identification of patients but for the orderly progress of the research being done around the world. Standards must be formed and maintained in order for one set of studies, in Japan, for instance, to be relevant to another set being carried out in Greece. Four different organizations came to the conference with their own sets of rules, referred to as the Copenhagen, Japanese, Greek, and California criteria[68]. Each was discussed separately and comparatively assessed with the goal of choosing the factors needed to make a single code to be used by all doctors and researchers. Dr.

---

[68]Rolf Manthorpe et al "The Copenhagen Criteria for Sjögren's Syndrome" *The Scandinavian Journal of Rheuatology 1986; Suppl. 61:* pp31-35

Manthorpe headed a committee presenting comments on the four criteria

It was basic that the syndrome involved, by definition, the eyes, mouth, and joints. But research has shown that the disease is an autoimmune disorder encompassing many different organs of the body as well as the exocrine glands. All parts of the body dependent on lubricating secretions for proper functioning must be considered in the overall picture of Sjögren's syndrome. To evaluate these involvements, it was noted that several tests should be made for each organ, the number depending on how specific the available tests are. If a test had been devised that will give a particular result *only* if Sjögren's is present it alone would be sufficient. But at this date, most tests can give positive results from other causes. We have seen that allergy medications, among others, can cause both dry eyes and dry mouth. But if a patient tells the doctor she feels the dryness (subjective evidence), a scintigram shows decreased secretion, and a lip biopsy confirms the presence of lymphocytes, it points specifically to SS as the cause of the oral dryness. It is essential that all the study centers use the same methods of testing.

Similarly, the terminology must be standard. Much of the history of confusion about SS arises from the use of different terms with vague meanings. Dry eye has been called "xerosis" or "xerophthalmia", but the latter word is firmly identified with a lack of vitamin A, and the term now generally accepted is Henrik Sjögren's own cumbersome, but certainly specific, keratoconjuntivitis sicca. That one is easy to recognize in writing but just wait until you hear an experienced doctor rattle it off rapidly!

A third problem is the distinction between objective and subjective abnormalities. Not only do some patients report dryness when there is no definite indication in the tests, but other patients may have positive test factors without complaining of noticeable symptoms. Perhaps it has been so long since their eyes felt normal, they no longer remember what it was like. In Copenhagen, the doctors insist that only the abnormalities that can be measured accurately should be considered. In California, they use mostly the strict tests, but also look for symptoms of dry mouth, etc. In Japan and Greece, the patients must have complaints about the dry eyes and mouth in addition to the positive test scores. Blood tests and biopsies also carry different importance to the different investigators. The Japanese, Greek, and Californian criteria distinguish between a definite and probable diagnosis, while only the Copenhagen and the Greek groups separate primary from secondary SS. The symposium report concluded that, in addition to observing a unified set of criteria, the tests used and their normal ranges should be noted in any reports of studies published in future scientific journals. That way all of the knowledge being painstakingly accumulated will increase the total information.

The Criteria Compared

The Copenhagen Criteria: Primary Sjögren's syndrome occurs if patient has KCS (dry eyes) *and* xerostomia (dry mouth) but does not meet international criteria for another chronic inflammatory connective tissue disease. KCS and xerostomia each require abnormal test results from two of the three following tests.

•For KCS: 1. The Schirmer-I test, 2. The break up time (BUT), 3. The van Bijsterveld score (rose bengal staining).
•For xerostomia: 1. Unstimulated sialogram, 2. Salivary gland scintigram, 3. Lower lip biopsy. [69]

The Greek Criteria: Definite primary SS requires two out of three of the following:
•For KCS: Patient complains of eyes feeling dry, Schirmer's test abnormal, or positive rose-bengal staining.
•For xerostomia: Patient complains of dry mouth, parotid flow rate is low, and the parotid glands are or have been swollen.
•All patients must have biopsy showing excess lymphocytes. [70]

The Japanese Criteria:
•For KCS: All patients must have symptoms of dry mouth plus positive rose-bengal and Schirmer's tests
•For xerostomia: All patients must have symptoms of dry eyes plus abnormal findings on lip biopsy and sialogram. [71]

The California Criteria:
•For KCS: Schirmer's test must show decreased tear flow and there must be increased staining with rose bengal or fluorescein dye.
•For xerostomia: Dry symptoms must be backed up by decreased salivary flow rates. A biopsy must show excessive lymphocytes

---

[69] Manthorpe "Copenhagen Criteria"

[70] F. Skopouli et al Preliminary Diagnostic Criteria for Sjögren's Syndrome" *The Scandinavian Journal of Rheumatology 1986; Suppl. 61:* pp22-25

[71] Mitsuo Homma et al "Criteria for Sjögren's Syndrome in Japan" *The Scandinavian Journal of Rheumatology 1986; Suppl. 61:* pp26-27

•Laboratory evidence of a systemic autoimmune disease. [72]

The overlapping and confusing elements of these criteria sets are graphically shown on Figure 11. Since the criteria generally do agree on the presence of dry eyes and dry mouth as important to the diagnosis, these are the first areas that will be tested once a patient has confessed to not liking saltines and having eye problems. But even the various tests now in use can be problematical. J. M. Gumpel put it well in his comments in the British Medical Journal.[73] "The results of diagnostic tests for Sjögren's syndrome," he says, "tend to be positive when the diagnosis is obvious, and equivocal when one most needs them."

The European Study Committee

Nevertheless, the effort continues to define Sjögren's syndrome. The Epidemiology Committee of the Commission of European Communities sponsored a workshop held in Pisa, Italy, in 1988, devoted entirely to the diagnosis of Sjögren's syndrome. Twenty-eight scientists from eleven European countries met to discuss related subjects and attempt to set up a standard for the disease. An entire issue of the journal *Clinical and Experimental Rheumatology* was devoted to this conference. The meeting resulted in a questionnaire and a manual to be used by physicians in making a diagnosis of Sjögren's syndrome. The extensive original questionnaire

[72]Robert Fox et al "First International Symposium on Sjögren's Syndrome: Suggested Criteria for Classification " *The Scandinavian Journal of Rheumatology* 1986; Suppl. 61: pp28-30

[73]J. Gumpel "Sjögren's Syndrome" *British Medical Journal* 4 December 1982; 285: 6355, p1598

was boiled down to six questions which its designers feel form a specific and sensitive test for SS.

2nd International SS Symposium - Austin

Just a few weeks later at the 2nd International Sjögren's Syndrome Symposium in Austin, Texas, shortly after *Sjögren's Syndrome: the Sneaky "Arthritis"* was published, further discussion of uniform criteria was held but without firm results. One suggestion was that presence of the SS-A or -B antibodies be made the sole criteria, but this was generally rejected.

3rd International SS Symposium - Ioannina

In June of 1991, at the 3rd symposium in Ioannina, Greece, Dr. Stefano Bombardieri reported on the work done by the European Study Committee. At that same conference, I presented a paper based on the letters readers have sent describing problems with Sjögren's Syndrome. A computerized database of the symptoms reported gave an interesting perspective on the great variety of problems encountered by Sjögren's Syndrome patients. The thrust of my discussion was that there was a great need for an extensive study of the symptoms that affect Sjögren's Syndrome patients. This larger study has been started in 1993.

Focus op Sjögren's, detailing a survey of 520 patients in the Netherlands was published in September of 1991. Twenty-two symptoms were counted, along with ages, associated diseases, and treatments. This study used criteria established by Drs. Troy Daniels and Norman Talal.[74]

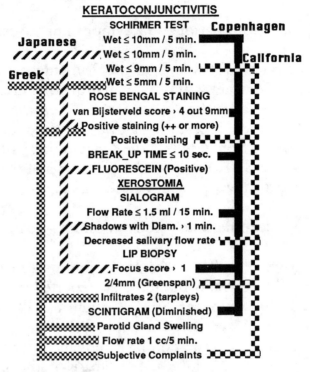

Figure 11 Criteria as Discussed at the 1st International Sjögren's Syndrome Symposium in Copenhagen, 1986

The European Study Group published their[75] criteria, which began with six simple questions about dry eyes and mouth for the first selection and was followed

[74]Troy E. Daniels and Norman Talal "Diagnosis and differential diagnosis of Sjögren's syndrome" Sjögren's syndrome: Clinical and immunological aspects, Springer-Verlag: 1987

[75]Claudio Vitali et al "Preliminary Criteria for the Classification of Sjögren's syndrome" Arthritis and Rheumatism

by tests including Schirmer, lactoferrin count, BUT, and rose bengal for the eyes; stimulated and unstimulated salivary flow rates, lip biopsy, scintography, and sialography for the mouth; and blood tests for RA factor, ANA, anti-Ro and anti-La. The suggested scores for these tests follow closely the Copenhagen Criteria shown on our chart (Figure 11), but with a more strict Schirmer score and with the addition of the requirement for at least one of the antibodies to be present. The latter condition had been included as an additional part of the California Criteria, though not shown on the chart.

The various sets of criteria have been refined and tuned since 1986 but are still not in full agreement.[76]

Diagnostic Procedures

Dry Eyes - Keratoconjunctivitis

For the eyes, two major tests will be administered by your ophthalmologist. First, the Schirmer test consists of placing short strips of filter paper inside the lower eyelid. This, as you might imagine, smarts, as it is intended to. The measurement depends on the amount of tears produced and the resulting wetness of the filter paper. A length of wetness of less than 5 millimeters is considered abnormal and an indication of SS.

---

[76]Robert Fox, Edward K. Chan and Ho-il Kang "Laboratory Evaluation of Patients with Sjögren's Syndrome" *Clinical Biochemistry* Vol. 25 pp.213-222, 1992

A more accurate test is the rose bengal staining method in which dye is placed in the eye and it is examined through a slit lamp. That's

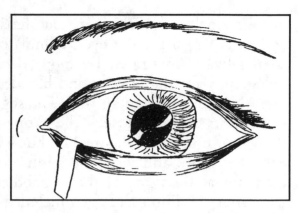

Figure 12 Schirmer Test

that devilishly bright light the doctor shines in your eyes so he can see what's going on. The stain takes better on damaged surfaces so the amount of staining he sees tells him the degree of dryness.

Still another test measures the length of time the tear film lasts between blinks. Normally it should be at least 15 seconds before the film begins to break up and dry spots appear. This breakup time (BUT) is also checked during a slit lamp examination.

Dry Mouth - Xerostomia

The involvement of the salivary glands is determined by a combination of observation and tests. Swellings of the glands along the cheekline can be more or less obvious and the inside of the mouth can be seen to be dry. Nuclear scanning measures the function of all the major salivary glands accurately and painlessly. Injections of dye can also be useful for X raying the parotid glands.

Scinti-scans use isotopes to identify a malfunctioning gland. The most effective confirmation of an oral Sjögren's syndrome diagnosis comes from a tissue sample (biopsy) of the saliva glands found on the inside of the lower lip. This can be examined under a microscope where the infiltrating lymphocytes can be counted.[77] When 50 or more inflammatory cells are found in a 4 millimeter square section of glandular tissue, the tissue is said to have a focus score of one, Anything greater than one is considered abnormal, and an indication of SS.[78] The researchers at the National Institute of Dental Research have developed still better methods of testing the salivary glands. They can now measure the flow of saliva from glands that have been stimulated by chewing or sucking on sour candies, etc., and can compare that with the flow when glands have not been stimulated, such as when sleeping or resting. A contraption called a periotron measures the electrical resistance of tiny amounts of saliva collected on a small piece of filter paper, providing a digital readout of the amount of saliva put out by one gland in 2 minutes. They also analyze the chemical makeup of the saliva to discover the reasons for the dryness. And blood tests can reveal the presence of antibodies, autoantibodies, and various markers that point to SS. All too often the first clue we have is the painful messages we get from our too rapidly decaying teeth.

There are, of course, many possible causes other than Sjögren's syndrome for a dry mouth and these must be eliminated for a firm diagnosis. More than 300

[77] L. Anderson, Norman Talal "The Spectrum of Benign to Malignant Lymphoproliferation in Sjögren's Syndrome" Clinical Experimental Immunology 1971; 9: 199-221

[78] M. Segerberg-Konttinen et al "Focus Score in the Diagnosis of Sjögren's Syndrome" Scandinavian Journal of Rheumatology 1986; Suppl. 61: 22-25

different medications have dryness of the mouth as a side effect.[79]

Accutrim	Diuril	Nicotine
Actifed	Ditropan	Nitrous Oxide
Aldoril	Donnatal	Parsidol
Aldomet	Dristan	Polaramine
Artane	Elavil	Primatine
Benadryl	Four Way Nasal Spray	Pro-Banthine
Caffeine	Halcion	Pyridium
Caladryl	Haldol	Quarzan
Cogentin	Inderal	Ru-Tuss
Combid	Inderide	Serpasil
Compazine	Laradopa	Thorazine
Comtrex	Lasix	Tofranil
Dalmane	Marijuana	Triaminic
Dexatrim	Max Strength Midol	Unisom
Diazide	Moban	Valium
Dimetane	Morphine	Vistrax

Figure 13 Some Medications That May Cause Dry
Eyes or Mouth

Particularly included among these are the blood pressure drugs, antidepressants, diet pills, antihistamines, tranquilizers, some Parkinson's disease drugs and some painkillers. Radiation or chemotherapy treatments for cancer can cause dryness, as can other diseases and conditions such as nutritional deficiencies and bone marrow transplants. It would be a mistake to assume any one cause for the problem without proper

---

[79]National Institute of Dental Research *Dry Mouth (Xerostomia)* Bethesda MD pamphlet

diagnostic testing, though it has been all too commonly done in the past. It is also important to mention here that the tests are not infallible and should be repeated for a follow-up. A negative Schirmer test or lip biopsy can be followed later by a positive test and many factors must be taken into consideration.

Arthritis

Examination for the (usually) relatively mild joint pains that accompany primary SS may be mostly subjective. That is the patient telling the doctor the extent of his or her aches and pains. But the doctor will want to pursue this by ordering blood tests to check for the presence of rheumatoid factors or antinuclear antibodies. These are the indicators for rheumatoid arthritis and lupus, respectively, and are frequently present in numbers too small to count as having the disease. The antibodies known as SS-A and SS-B are signals for a diagnosis of Sjögren's syndrome.

Extraglandular

Other tests to check for involvement of specific organs may be needed. These may include, for example, urine tests for kidney function, chest X rays to examine lungs, or thyroid function tests. A relatively new technique, magnetic resonance imaging, is an extremely sensitive procedure for detecting signs of nervous system involvement and distinguishing SS/CNS from the diseases it tends to mimic; multiple sclerosis, Alzheimer's, and Parkinson's.[80] This is important, since,

---

[80]Talal *Sjögren's Syndrome,*

according to Dr. Elaine Alexander, unlike those other cases, the memory problems of SS are potentially treatable if diagnosed early.

Secondary Sjögren's Syndrome

However, as we have noted before, about 50 percent of all SS patients have some form of connective tissue disease along with their SS, so it is important to establish the presence or absence of another disease. Generally, it has been observed that in secondary SS, the other disease is noticed and diagnosed first, but a patient should always be observed for any changes that develop during treatment.

Rheumatoid Arthritis

The most common associated disease is rheumatoid arthritis and since it, like SS, affects the body many ways, it can take a combination of methods and possibly a fair amount of time to arrive at a firm diagnosis. The doctor will study your affected joints for signs of swelling, inflammation, or distortion. In addition to checking your blood for RA factor, he may order a sed rate (erythrocyte sedimentation rate) test which measures the speed with which the red blood cells sink to the bottom of a test tube. RA patients have a faster rate of fall than others. During this same lab workup, your blood will probably be checked for red cell count or anemia. There may be other tests made from blood or urine and though X rays tend not to show any abnormalities at the beginning, they may be taken to serve as a measure for changes later.

Lupus

The second most common associated disease is lupus (systemic lupus erythematosus or SLE.) This one is even more complicated than RA to diagnose. Similar blood tests will be done, this time looking for the ANA (antinuclear antibody) proteins that are a marker for lupus. Essentially the same tests as for RA will be done plus, possibly, chest X rays and an electrocardiogram. If the doctor thinks the kidneys may be involved, he may order a biopsy of that organ.

Scleroderma

A few SS patients also have scleroderma. Tests specifically designed to establish the presence of scleroderma may include a skin biopsy and a check of the muscle pressure of your esophagus to measure digestive system involvement, if any. Blood work is needed here also, and since scleroderma is complicated, some patients may be asked to enter the hospital for a short stay for more diagnostic tests.

Chapter 6 - Treatment

By this time you may be wondering, what's the point? Arthritis is chronic and incurable, right? So's this Sjögren's syndrome thing. So why go to all this bother to figure out what you've got or which one you've got? Reading about all these symptoms just makes it worse and all those tests are an expensive nuisance. Maybe we'd all be better off not knowing. I hate needles anyway.

True, there is, at this point, no cure for Sjögren's syndrome, or any of the related connective tissue diseases. But there are ways to treat the symptoms and prevent or alleviate the consequences.

The care program that you and your doctor will work out can be broken down into three areas. A combination of medication, careful observation and exercise, specifically tailored for your needs, will help you feel better and make life easier for you.

Dry Eyes

The most important thing for your eyes is to protect them from irritation by replacing the moisture the tear glands can no longer supply. For this we use artificial tears. There is an assortment of non-prescription artificial tears available at your local drug store. Some are methylcellulose based and some use polyvinyl alcohol, while others are made up of combinations of these or other ingredients. The are more than thirty different brands of artificial tear drops, most of which are available without prescription. The choice is not always easy. As Dr. Herbert Kaufman writes in *International Ophthalmological Clinic*[81] "Selecting artificial tears on a logical basis does not work." Since every patient is different, most ophthalmologists recommend a trial and error process for finding the best drops for your eyes. The ophthalmologist may give you samples and tell you to experiment, or your pharmacist can help you choose. There are basically three different types of artificial tears: hypotonic (less concentrated than natural tears), plain saline, and those containing polymers. The same variety applies to the frequency of using the drops. Generally they are to be used, as needed, about four times a day for mild cases, more for severe irritations. If they are needed often, the eyes may become sensitive to preservatives in the drops and a switch would be indicated to drops using a different preservative or one of the preservative-free types. The latter should be used carefully, since there is more danger of bacterial contamination, which could cause infections. Preservative-free drops, often identified by the words PF, generally come in single-dose containers or must be kept refrigerated after opening. The single dose containers are small plastic vials usually about 2 inches long with a twist off top. The manufacturers state that they should be discarded after each use even though they contain enough tears for more than one use. Several brands are available, some of which are listed here.

---

[81]Kaufman *Keratitis Sicca* pp133-143

Tear Name	Manufacturer
Aquasite	CIBAVision
Bion Tears	Alcon
Cellufresh	Allergan
Hypo Tears PF	Iolab
Tears Naturale Free	Alcon

Figure 14 Some Preservative-Free Tears

Bion Tears, introduced in 1993 include a special bicarbonate element, which according to Dr. J. Daniel Nelson of the St. Paul - Ramsey Medical Center in Minneapolis and his colleagues, provides improvement in test results as well as symptoms of discomfort and dryness. The bicarbonate is said to form a gel on the eye's surface, similar to the gel that protects the stomach lining.

Often any drops you take in the daytime are not sufficient to last through the night, in which case there are ointments available which, when placed in the eyes, will sustain the moisturizing action until morning. Some people object to these, however, as they form a thick scummy coating that causes blurry vision and must be washed out in the morning. There is also available a slow-release insert (Lacri-sert) as a night application. Tiny pellets are placed under the lower lid, using a special applicator. They absorb moisture, swell, and gradually release lubricants over a long period. These pellets have some disadvantages, though, in that they are expensive and for some people who may not produce enough tears to dissolve them, the pellets may cause a feeling of something solid in the eye. I cannot use pellets so I keep a supply of drops on the night stand by my bed. I wake frequently during the night and it's easier not to have to get up and hunt for them.

Where these methods are just not enough, other options include mucus-dispersing (mucolytic) drops, humidifiers to minimize dryness in the air, blocking of the tear drainage channels (punctal occlusion), or the use of soft contact lenses to help hold in the moisture.

Dr. Kasuo Tsubota of Tokyo has studied the protective effects of glasses and recommends wearing them to help maintain the environmental moisture level of the eyes. He suggests glasses with side panels for maximum protection and stresses the need to wear them in conditions of wind or artificial heat.[82] For greater moisture preservation, it is possible to have plastic panels fitted to your glasses and your face to form moisture chambers. Tsubota's studies show that even dry eye patients had 20% more humidity when wearing glasses with side panels. In the original version of this book, I reported, somewhat facetiously, about one enterprising inventor who created a pair of glasses with a built-in reservoir of tears that run through a little trough into the eyes.[83] Then in 1992, Dr. James Bertera, of Scheppens Eye Reseaech Institute described a new type of reservoir glasses with a delivery system based on an adaptation of the ink jet method used in some computer printers. [84]

---

[82]Kasuo Tsubota "The Effect of Wearing Spectacles on the Humidity of the Eye " *American Journal of Ophthalmology*, Vol. 108, #1, July 15, 1989

[83]Shearn *Sjögren's Syndrome* p201

[84]James Bertera "Simulation of Lacrimal Gland Output: A tear Jet System for Projecting Fluids onto the Ocular Surface" Program and Abstract Book, International Conference on the Lacrimal Gland tear film and Dry Eye Syndromes: November 14-17 1992, Southampton Parish, Bermuda

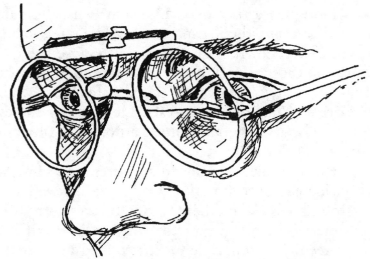

Figure 15 Reservoir Glasses (original)

Punctal occlusion is used to accomplish a reverse of this idea. The puncta are ducts in the inner corner of the eyes. They are designed to allow excess fluid to drain from the eyes into the nasal ducts and eventually to the throat. For Sjögren's patients who can't afford to lose any of the precious moisture, a possible solution is to block these ducts, to retain the tears in the eyes. This can help but is sometimes only a temporary relief.

Usually your ophthalmologist will suggest placing plugs in the lower puncta first. If called for, the upper ducts may be closed also. These are generally temporary plugs such as those made of collagen by Eagle Vision. They act like plugs in a bathtub and allow the patient and doctor to decide if stopping up the ducts helps. The collagen dissolves in the duct after four to seven days and the ducts may then be closed by a more permanent method. The Herrick Lacrimal plug is one example of the type made of non-dissolving silicone and looks like a miniature golf tee. Eagle Vision's Freeman plug is shaped more like a tiny rivet. Insertion is usually pain-less but a local anesthetic can be used. The plugs can be removed if needed. It is also possible to close the duct entrance by cautery or adhesives. These procedures can be enough to solve the dry eye problem for those whose glands are still making some tears. Of course if the eye is completely dry (the gland makes no tears) plugging the drain will not help.

None of the steps mentioned are cures, and some are still considered controversial or may have disadvantages. Wraparound glasses help keep drying breezes away from the eyeballs, but are illegal to wear while driving in some states. The contact lenses prescribed as a sort of bandage for the eye, may cause as much irritation and infection for some people as they are designed to pre-vent. It is important to remember that your ophthal-mologist is the only one who can properly assess the condition of your eyes and the best means of treating them. It is essential to have regular examinations, as more serious problems such as scratching of the eye cov-ering (corneal abrasion) and infections may result from the lack of sufficient tears.

If light sensitivity is a problem, use of sunglasses with ultraviolet protection and avoidance of excess exposure may be called for. Some patients who are bothered by light, wear "wrap-around" sunglasses with the side panels. Extremely dry environments can aggravate the symptoms and should be either avoided or compensated for. Watertight swim goggles can help hold in the moisture. I add a face mask for protection when work-ing on a project that involves sawdust in the air. Some medications taken for other problems, such as decongest-ants for a cold, have a drying effect, important to con-sider when taking over-the-counter cold tablets. Also it pays to make sure any other doctor you see is aware that you have Sjögren's so he can make proper judgements about prescribing certain medications that have dryness as a side effect. As with any other aspect of arthritis there are continuing efforts to find new and better cures. Some are genuine scientific studies and some, such as offbeat diet quirks, are sheer nonsense. Be aware that any true advances come only after carefully conducted trials and investigations. Some studies now being carried out in ophthalmology include the use of topical Vitamin A tear pumps that can be implanted directly in the eye to supply tears, and a surgical transplant of salivary duct tissue to the tear gland. One idea being used is the concoction of tear drops using the patient's own blood serum.[85] These are effective but expensive and inconvenient since they use no preservatives. They must be made fresh by drawing blood periodically, and must be kept frozen. Gel tears, Healon (hyaluronic acid),[86] and drugs (Bromhexine hydrochloride) to stimulate tear production are under investigation.

In using artificial tears several precautions need to be considered. Foremost is the need to use drops frequently. Don't wait until your eyes hurt; establish a regular routine. Watch for signs of irritation or possible infection. Be careful not to contaminate your eyes or the dropper. Avoid or protect against drying environments. And be sure to discuss any changes in medication or condition with your ophthalmologist.

[85]Norman Talal " Sjögren's Syndrome and Connective Tissue Disease with other Immunological Disorders" McCarty *Arthritis and Related Conditions* Philadelphia: Lea & Febiger; 1985-87

[86]V. DeLuise, W. Peterson "The Use of Topical Healon™ Tears in the Management of Refactory Dry-eye Syndrome" *Annals of Ophthalmology* September 1984: 823-824

Dry Mouth

Many of the same concerns are applicable to the problem of a dry mouth in Sjögren's syndrome. Once again, little can be done to reverse the damage of Sjögren's, but much to alleviate and prevent. As with the eyes, the primary concern is to replace lost moisture. The obvious solution is simply to drink more water. Keeping a glass handy and just sipping on it as needed relieves the uncomfortable sensation of dryness in the mouth and throat. This is especially important when you have to talk a lot. Those long conversations on the telephone can be trying if you don't have a drink handy. Soft drinks are OK but they should be sugar-free. Not only does sugar present a danger of decay for the teeth, but it draws moisture out of the mouth tissues (by osmosis). Often a thicker drink gives more comfort, and for this tomato juice is good. My greatest temptation is to eat ice cream or drink milkshakes, but this habit, carried on frequently during the day, can have disastrous results on the figure.

Sugar-free gelatin helps, but when you can't have a glass or dish of it handy, sugar-free lozenges, mints, or chewing gum can save the day. They stimulate the ailing glands to produce more saliva. Some people swear by sourball candy, so much so that one doctor has suggested that as a diagnostic tool. A piece of lemon rind or a cherry pit held in the mouth has the same potential to stimulate activity from a recalcitrant saliva gland,[87] but that seems like cruel and unusual punish-

---

[87]Morgan *"Mikulicz's Disease"* p471

Figure 16 Too Many Milkshakes!

ment to me. And in fact, some doctors have expressed concern that the acidity of the lemon could be harmful to some patients.

I always keep a glass of water (or other liquid) at my desk as I write and put one right next to my eye drops on the night stand by my bed. One patient came up with the suggestion to keep grapes handy to suck on.

Figure 17 Lemon peel Stimulating Saliva

She keeps some in the freezer for added pizzazz. I also need to have some liquid with food at meals to help the mouthfuls slide along their way.

There are commercially available saliva substitutes (Salivart, Xero-Lube, MouthKote, Roxane and others previously mentioned) but they cannot completely duplicate the natural saliva. If your lips are dry or the corners of your mouth crack, they can be relieved with chapped lip sticks such as Chapstick. For an added benefit, Hawaiian Tropic makes a lip balm that contains a 15 spf sunblock. If the irritation (cheilitis) is caused by a yeast infection (candidiasis), more aggressive treatment with anti-fungal creams such as Mycelex (containing the drug clotrinazole) or Nystatin may be needed.. Your tongue may tend to crack and therefore, be extra sensitive to spicy or acid foods[88] I am constantly being told by "civilians" that such and such a food is "not hot at all", but even a trace of that jalapeno pepper Texans love so can burn my tender tongue. Just by natural selection I avoid citrus fruits and highly seasoned foods. All this is not in your imagination. You are short of the mucins in normal saliva that protect against irritants in food. Ulcers inside the mouth can sometimes be soothed by warm baking soda rinses.[89] Sara Endress reports that Borafax, applied to her lips at night, eases the dryness and protects them from getting sore. A bendable straw for her bedside drinking glass keeps it from being washed away with each sip. She uses Moistir and Moistir-10 spray for her throat and mouth just before retiring. There is also a gel called Oralbalance from Laclede Professional Products, which can be

---

[88]Papathanasiou *Respiratory Abnormalities in SS* pp370-374

[89]W. Wright "Oral Health Care Program Recommended by National Institute of Dental Research of NIH" *Moisture Seekers Newsletter* Great Neck NY January 1987; 4: 1, pp1-2

helpful for the dry mouth that comes in the night. I squeeze about 3/8 inch of the stuff on my tongue and swish it around to coat my mouth, and this gives considerable relief.

Protecting Teeth

In all this, I avoid excessive sugar for the sake of my teeth. If excessive sugar and teeth add up to decay in the average person, think what they do to us Sjögren's syndrome sufferers. Since the teeth are at great risk for the Sjögren's patient, it is important to have regular and frequent checkups (at least every three months) with your dentist and to be sure he knows about your Sjögren's. There are several problems here, one being that food sticks more firmly to the teeth. For this reason, careful cleaning and flossing is essential. But beyond that, certain ingredients in normal saliva are lacking that would protect the teeth against decay. Your dentist may suggest the use of fluoride as a rinse. As in normal dental care, the best cure is prevention. This is especially true with Sjögren's syndrome, making one of the most emphatic points for the value of early diagnosis. Being forewarned, in this case, is being forearmed, and meticulous attention to care and cleaning may help save your teeth.

For this, Biotene toothpaste and chewing gum (also by Laclede) may be helpful. The formula includes an antibacterial ingredient to reduce gum irritation and plaque. Viadent toothpaste is also designed to reduce plaque. Sensodyne toothpaste, by Block Drug Company can help against the pain of sensitive teeth.

A variety of mouthwashes are available. Some contain fluoride (Colgate's Fluorigard, Johnson &

Johnson's ACT), others are aimed at controlling plaque (Omnii International's Omnii, Plax, Viadent, Biotene). Peridex, available by prescription only, contains chlorhexidine which helps heal sore and bleeding gums. PreviDent Gel-Tin, NeutraCare, and Omnii Med are fluoride gels to be applied after brushing and before bedtime to increase the protective effect of other fluoride treatments. For even more protection, your dentist can make a tray to fill with fluoride and place in your mouth while sleeping. At least one person who uses this method tells me he doesn't notice that it's there.

Dental Implants

Of course, as about forty million Americans (with or without SS) know, that happy ending doesn't always happen. When, in spite of our best efforts, the teeth go, one by one or with SS even faster, we enter into a desperate struggle with the forces of destiny. Most SS patients will be familiar with the steps of this process. As youngsters, we probably had regular, semiannual visits to the dentist. Instead of "Look, Ma, no cavities!", we would come home with a report of several new fillings added to our collection. Eventually, possibly shortly after we have had our first baby, we lose our first tooth. Regularly, we get lectures from our dental technician about all the preferred methods of defeating the dreaded plaque. Increasingly, we have larger and larger fillings and, soon, root canals, crowns and partial dentures to replace unsavable teeth. A caring dentist will go to great lengths to save the teeth that insist on crumbling despite our best efforts. Finally, when all else fails, we allow our dentist to extract the remaining teeth on, for instance, our lower jaw. This of course requires a full removeable denture. Drs. Jane Atkinson and Philip Fox at the National Institute of Dental Research in Bethesda, Maryland, have done considerable research into this problem and have concluded that "There is no evidence that patients with SS are any more dissatisfied with complete dentures than patients with normal salivary function." They point out that the attitude of the patient influences the success of dentures. "Telling patients with SS they will never adapt to removeable prostheses," they say "is not in the best interest of the patient."[90] This may well be the case, but for those of us who do not share this happy experience, there is another solution.

In some cases, dentures can be a real pain, literally. A shortage of saliva affects the patient's ability to wear dentures in several ways. The most obvious is the lack of lubrication. Dentures sitting on dry gums can cause irritation and sores that can be quite painful as well as bringing the chance of infection. Bits of food stuck under the plates are also annoying and uncomfortable. Since the gums may shrink the dentures may become loose and slip, making all of the above problems worse. In addition, this affects the ability to chew and promotes a tendency to swallow foods not properly prepared. When all these problems are severe, it often leads to reluctance to wear the dentures. It can be very embarrassing to get halfway to an important meeting, only to realize that you have forgotten to put your teeth in!

In the late forties, dentists began working on a solution to all this distress. They experimented with the

[90]Jane Atkinson and Philip Fox "Sjögren's Syndrome: Oral and Dental Considerations" *Journal of American Dental Association*, Vol 124 March 1993 pp74-84

idea of implanting supports into the jaw to hold replacements for our lost natural teeth. Why not put metal "studs" directly into the bones of the jaw to hold the dentures or even individual teeth firmly? Actually, this was not a new idea. Archeologists in Egypt have found jawbones with precious stones and metal apparently meant to replace lost teeth. The Mayans used carved seashells for the same purpose.[91] But early modern efforts had problems with design, materials and safety monitoring.

When I reached this stage in the mid 80s the work was still considered experimental and risky. Problems arose with infections caused by the metals used and the fact that they protruded through the gums allowing bacteria to reach the bone. Patients complained of pain from the implants. My dentist advised against it for me at that time. But research continued and new methods and materials were developed that have made the process much safer and more satisfactory for many patients

Three different systems evolved. The endosseous (in the bone) implant resemble small (very small) screws anchored firmly in the bone to support a fixed bridge. Subperiosteal (under the gum) implants use a metal framework placed between the bone and the gum tissue. In the third type, the staple bone plate implant or transosseous (through the bone), a plate is placed on the underside of the jaw with the posts passing through the bone and the gums to hold the denture.[92]

The most commonly used of these is a system developed by a Swedish orthopedic surgeon, Dr. P. I.

[91]"Dental Implants, Replants, and transplants" *Broadening the Scope* National Institute oif Dental Research

[92]Albert D. Guckes "Dental Implants" *National Institutes of Health Concensus Development Conference Statement* Vol. 7, #3, June 15, 1988

Brånemark. In this procedure, from 4 to 6 titanium cylinders are implanted into the jaw bone and the gum is allowed to heal over them. In four to six months (or in some cases a bit longer) the bone will have grown into indentations in the metal, firmly fixing it into the bone structure. A second surgery is then needed to attach posts that will stick out of the gums. When this has healed, a permanent denture made of metal and ceramic is made to order for the patient and permanently attached to the posts. These can actually be removed if necessary by the dentist as they are held in with tiny screws, but are not like ordinary dentures that must be taken out each night.

This, as must be obvious, is not an easy process. While the surgery is generally conducted in the dentist's office under local anesthesia, there can be considerable discomfort during the healing process. The dentures that you have been wearing are even less comfortable and effective during this time than before the surgery. And since SS patients sometimes heal slowly, it can be a rather long, drawn out process. In my case, it took just over a year from start to finish. And it is an expensive procedure, not often covered by medical insurance. But—and this is a big but—the rewards are great. Once your implants are in place you can chew your food, and enjoy it without pain. And, assuming you follow your doctor's advice about dental hygiene, which must be even more stringent than before, your new teeth should be trouble free. At last you can say, "look Ma, no cavities!"

It is also possible, and often practical to have partial or single tooth implants which can be part of an ongoing plan for a particular patient's care. In one instance for me, a single tooth repair, using root canal, surgery and crown, was almost as expensive and time consuming as an implant would have been. So it is wise, if you have SS and can more or less expect to have extensive loss of teeth, to look to the future and plan with your oral care specialists (dentist, endodontist, periodontist and surgeon) to consider the overall picture.

Research continues in the area of dental implants and there should be improvements in methods, materials and economy as time passes. A brighter future is coming for SS patients with severe dental problems.

Swollen Glands

The swollen salivary (parotid) glands of SS may be a cosmetic problem that the patient must simply grin and bear (difficult as that may be with such a puffy face!). If the gland damage is more severe, treatment may take the form of medication with corticosteroids, cytotoxic drugs like those used in chemotherapy for cancer, or X-ray treatments.[93]As these potent procedures may have serious side effects, they are used only with caution and in severe cases. Some physicians will suggest that the disabled glands be surgically removed, but I would always ask for a second opinion on this. There is also the thought that if the glands function at all, they should be saved and encouraged.

Arthritis

The joint pains that often accompany primary Sjögren's syndrome are usually mild (although there are some who would dispute that statement) and can be successfully treated with aspirin or anti-inflammatory

---

[93]Talal *Recognize and Treat Sjögren's Syndrome* pp80-87

drugs (NSAIDs). These drugs do their magic in two ways. They can make you feel better by alleviating the pain of your joints, and they can prevent (or at least, slow down) the damage by helping to reduce inflammation, the source of the pain. Since these drugs can also have side effects, they must be carefully selected by your doctor in what may sometimes be a tedious and frustrating trial and error process. There are a great variety of these drugs and they have different results with different people. One type might suppress your inflammation and pain nicely, but irritate your digestive system to a dangerous degree, while another might be totally ineffective for you.

The doctor can analyze benefits and possible side effects to suit your needs, but often a particular medication will require a trial run to determine if it is suitable for you. *Under no circumstances* should the patient attempt to choose his own medications or adjust them without the doctors concurrence. This information and what follows is included here only so that the patient may give informed consent to the regime his doctor suggests.

The Systemic Approach

By now, we know that the SS triad is only part of the story. Treating the specific afflictions of dry eyes, mouth and joints often cannot solve all the problems. Drugs that can give general relief, such as aspirin or NSAIDs are systemic drugs. A humorous poem published in a support group newsletter asked the question, "How does the pill know where to go?" The systemic

SIDE EFFECTS \ DRUGS	BUTAZOLIDINE	TOLECTIN	NAPROSYN	NALFON	MOTRIN	MECLOMEN	INDOCIN	FELDENE	CLINORIL	TRILISATE	ASPIRIN
INDIGESTION (GAS)	X	X	X	X	X	X	X	X	X		X
STOMACH IRRITATION	X	X	X	X	X		X	X	X		X
NAUSEA	X	X	X	X	X	X	X	X	X	X	X
HEARTBURN	X	X	X	X	X	X	X	X	X		
PEPTIC ULCERS								X			X
CONSTIPATION									X		
DIARRHEA						X					
STOMACH PAIN								X			
VOMITING										X	X
FLUID RETENTION	X	X	X	X	X			X	X		
WEIGHT GAIN	X										
ASCEPTIC MENINGITIS						X					
STIFF NECK						X					
FEVER						X					
NERVOUSNESS								X			
CONFUSION							X				
ITCHING								X			
RASH	X	X	X					X			
RINGING EARS									X	X	X
HEARING LOSS										X	X
BLOOD THINNING											X
LIVER DAMAGE											X
ALLERGIES	X	X	X	X	X		X	X	X	X	X
RAPID BREATHING										X	X
LOSS OF WHITE CELLS	X										
LOSS OF RED CELLS	X										
HEADACHE					X		X		X		

Figure 18 NSAIDs With Side Effects

drugs don't care. They just set out to fix the whole ball game.

And when those drugs are not enough to do the job, there are others that are stronger or just work in different ways. In some cases steroids or immunosuppressive drugs may be needed but these powerful drugs are prescribed with great caution. Many have important side effects, so the doctor must weigh with you the

NSAIDs	Cortico-Steroids	Disease Modifiers
Aspirin	Cortisone	
Disalcid, Trilisate	prednisone	Plaquenil
Naproxen Ansaid	Medrol (methyl prednisolone	Imuran (Gold)
Clinoril		**Immunosuppressives**
Ibuprofen (Advil, Nuprin)		Methotrexate
Indocin		Cyclosporin A
Voltaren		Penicillamine

Figure 19 **Some Drugs For SS Treatment**

balance of risk versus benefit. This ratio is seldom cut and dried and often has to be determined individually for each patient. You will find much difference of opinion among individual doctors and in the research literature. [94]

---

[94]Robert Fox "Treatment of the Patient with Sjögren's Syndrome" *Rheumatic Disease Clinics of North America: Sjögren's Syndrome* Vol 18, Number 3 August 1992 p707

Steroids

The term steroids includes a large category of substances created by the body or synthesized by man. Among them are cholesterol, D vitamins, bile acids, sex hormones, and the hormones secreted by the adrenal glands. [95] One of the latter, cortisone, was developed as a treatment for arthritis in the '50s. The drug was hailed as a miracle for arthritis patients and its discoverers, Philip S. Hench and Tadeus Reichstein were given the 1950 Nobel Prize for Medicine. All over the country, swollen joints subsided and pains faded away. Arthritis sufferers were ecstatic. For a while. But after a time, it became obvious that the panacea was not without its price. In fact some side effects outweighed the benefits.

Cortisone therapy increases the patient's supply of the hormones ordinarily produced by the adrenal glands. This helps to reduce inflammation and suppress immunologic responses. Beyond the mere reduction in pain, important as that is, cortisone (or the more commonly prescribed prednisone) seems to help retard the process in Sjögren's. That's the good part. But steroids have a down side that varies with the dosage and the length of time taken.

By far the majority of patients are given what are considered low doses, from 5 to 10 milligrams of prednisone per day. At this level the side effects are usually mild and can be tolerated or dealt with. Steroids may cause water retention with a resultant puffiness, especially around the face. (Remember Sjögren's can cause

[95]Norman Talal, L. Smith "Recent Clinical and Experimental Developments in Sjögren's Syndrome" *Western Journal of Medicine* January, 1975; 122: 50-58

puffy jaws even without the prednisone.) An increased appetite can lead to unwelcome weight gain. Fragility of tiny blood vessels under the skin (particularly on the forearms) can cause purplish-red (but painless) bruises that appear at the slightest bump or scraping of the skin. When these spots fade, they leave permanent brown stains (iron deposits) under the skin in their wake. The skin itself can become thin and tear easily. In this case the result is a white scar. These problems are mostly cosmetic and a nuisance and should not necessitate stopping the therapy. The thin skin can cause problems when surgery is needed, as it sometimes allows stitches to tear out and/or slows healing of the wound.

Other possible problems such as dizziness, flushing, restlessness, and indigestion can occur when you first start taking prednisone, but these will usually go away in a couple of weeks. More major are the dangers of ulcers, depression, calcium loss, cataracts, or inflammation of the arteries (vasculitis) that can come with high dosages and/or long use. It is therefore important for the patient to be a partner with his or her physician. The doctor should carefully explain the possible disadvantages as well as the benefits from the therapy proposed. In most cases the doctor will not recommend a treatment unless the benefits will be great and the risk justified. Doctors differ in their use of steroids and if you do not fully understand or agree with your doctor's suggestions, you might get a second opinion. Some doctors will suggest pulse therapy, that is, a larger dose given all at once by injection. This can avoid some of the side effects of longer term dosage.

One point your doctor will impress on you is that you must follow his directions explicitly. The medication must be taken exactly as indicated (i.e., one in the morning and one at night, etc.) and the quantity must not be changed without his approval. Prednisone suppresses the natural activity of the adrenal glands and they tend to dry up (atrophy). If prednisone is suddenly withdrawn, the glands need time to recover so as to resume production of the hormone. Otherwise, the body would be without it for a time. To avoid this when going off the drug, one must gradually decrease the dosage, allowing the natural gland to slowly recover. In some cases (such as when undergoing surgery even for an unrelated problem), you may need a temporarily increased supply of hormones. It is important that *any* doctor who sees or treats you, knows exactly what medications you are using.

Plaquenil

A drug originally used to combat malaria, Plaquenil (hydroxychloroquine sulfate) is classified as a disease-modifying drug. It does more than just make you feel better. Like the steroids, it can reduce inflammation. But this benefit carries with it an element of risk. In large doses it can cause damage to the retina and, in infrequent cases, can lead to blindness. But the limits of safe dosage have been pretty well established and as long as those limits are carefully observed, Plaquenil is now generally considered to be a safe drug. Dr. Howard N. Bernstein found no damage from Plaquenil in all the worldwide medical literature for 1975-89 or 1975-90 FDA reports among patients receiving up to 6.5 mg per kilogram of body weight for 10 years or less.[96] A patient taking more than that or for a longer period of time is watched very carefully, with eye exams every six months to check for such signs as reduced visual field. And the results are varied.

The American Medical Association reports "70% of rheumatoid arthritis patients experience moderate relief of symptoms."[97] One SS patient has told me she credits Plaquenil for a great improvement in her case. Others get little noticeable benefit. Because it is a slow-acting drug, if your doctor starts you on Plaquenil, it's important to give it at least a six months trial before deciding whether or not it's helping you.

Gold Compounds

It is not definitely known how they work but gold compounds have been used in cases where more conservative drugs haven't helped enough. They do have an anti-inflammatory effect, but even better, they appear to modify the disease. Originally gold was given only in painful injections but a newer form, auranofin (Ridaura) can be taken by mouth. It helps with morning stiffness, swollen joints, weakness, fatigue and unwanted weight loss. It can lower the sed rate and RA factor. It is both less effective and less toxic than the older versions of Gold therapy. Some of its adverse effects are intestinal disturbances (especially diarrhea), skin rashes, hair loss, and conjunctivitis.

---

[96]Howard N. Bernstein "Hydroxychloroquine: easy on the eyes?" *Arthritis Today* The Arthritis Foundation Atlanta GA Sept-Oct 1992

[97]AMA Directory of Drug Applications Spring 1990

Immunosuppressives

Immunosuppressive drugs (penicillamine, cyclosporin A) are even more powerful and dangerous than steroids, and so, are used with even more caution. Only in severe, life-threatening conditions are they called for. Immunosuppressives work by attacking rapidly dividing cells. In Sjögren's, the damage is caused by proliferating (rapidly dividing) lymphocytes. When these get out of hand, immunosuppressives can help keep them in check. These are the same drugs that we hear so much about for their lifesaving role in organ transplants. When the immune system goes to work to protect the body from the alien organ the doctors have foisted upon it, immunosuppressives restrain the system, allowing the transplanted organ to function properly in its new home. The problem here is that the drugs cannot always distinguish which cells they are supposed to attack, and healthy, necessary cells may be the target. Bone marrow cells, for instance, are also rapidly-dividing cells. Increased susceptibility to infection is another danger and it is suspected (though not proven) that long term use of these drugs could cause cancer. Obviously these risks mean that the drugs must be restricted to the most severe cases.

We have seen that some primary SS patients are highly subject to adverse reactions to treatment with gold salts or penicillamine. This does not seem to be true for those with secondary SS beyond what is to be expected with RA alone.

Observation

It is essential that your doctor keep close tabs on your

medications. He will set a schedule for office visits which should be strictly kept. You must carefully note any changes in your condition that may possibly be side effects of the drugs, and mention them to him. A list and/or marked drawings will be helpful (See Part II, Chapter I). It is sometimes hard to remember the aches and pains that plagued you yesterday when a myriad of new and different ones are competing for your attention today. It also can be trying for a doctor to listen attentively to a long vocal recital of these same complaints. A concisely stated list or a clear, simple representation on a drawing can tell him in a minute the pattern of your problems. DO NOT make any changes in your medications without first discussing them with your doctor. And feel free to call the doctor in between appointments if problems come up.

To supplement your subjective reporting, the doctor will do periodic blood workups. Many of the tests used to diagnose your Sjögren's syndrome (and any associated disease you may have) must be repeated periodically to monitor your progress. He will check on the number and volume of red and white blood cells and your sedimentation rate which measures the amount of inflammation. He may do a urinalysis to keep tabs on your kidneys. He will examine your mouth for visual evidence of dryness and irritation. There are, of course other tests to be employed for specific conditions.

Exercise

When your hips and knees hurt, the first thing you may think of is to turn on your favorite soap opera, stretch out on the sofa, and take it easy. The doctor did say get plenty of rest, didn't he? But research and good old common sense combine to tell you that kind of coddling's not the best way to treat those creaky joints. On the contrary, studies show that exercise, carefully chosen and moderately carried out, can be the best medicine. Octogenarian Dvera Berson says she has eliminated the pain of her severe arthritis by a long time regime of water exercises.[98] A look at the makeup of a typical joint will show you why that occurs. You will notice that the joint is a closed system. That is, it is enclosed within a capsule and lubricated by the fluid created within the synovial membrane. While most tissues of the body are served by arteries that bring them essential nutrients, there are no such arteries connecting to the joint cartilage. It receives all its nourishment through the synovial fluid which must be circulated within the joint to carry out its duty of providing the nutrients and carrying off wastes. Exercise creates the movement necessary for this circulation. Furthermore, as with healthy bodies, muscles must be exercised to keep their tone and their ability to keep us in motion. The old saying "Use it or lose it." applies especially to us.[99] Evidence shows that exercise helps maintain or improve the strength of bones by slowing calcium loss.

The Arthritis Foundation divides the 109 identified types of arthritis into eight major categories, of which we need be concerned generally with only two: synovitis and muscle inflammation. Synovitis, by the Foundation's definition, includes the conditions where an inflammation of the synovium causes the pain; the other category involves muscle inflammation. Sjögren's

[98]Dvera Berson, Sander Ray *Pain Free Arthritis* 1978 S & J Books, Brooklyn NYpg 9
[99]Kate Lorig, James Fries The Arthritis Helpbook 1980 Addison-Wesley Publishing Company; Reading, MA pp25-26

syndrome and its associated connective tissue diseases (rheumatoid arthritis, lupus, myositis, dermatomyositis, and scleroderma) fall into these two categories.[100] As we have seen, exercise will help alleviate the effects of these inflammatory states.

There are other ways in which exercise is thought to help. We think we feel pain in a particular location. Swollen finger joints ache dully or our hips may protest sharply against that bending over gardening we are determined to do. But what is actually happening is that messages are being sent to our brains where the

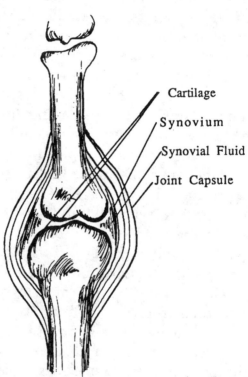

Cartilage

Synovium

Synovial Fluid

Joint Capsule

Figure 20 **Joint with Synovial Capsule**

pain receptors call attention to what is happening to the knuckles. This serves an important purpose, as when we put our hands on a hot pot, the pain signal swiftly tells us to let go, before any more harm is done.

---

[100]James Fries *Arthritis: A Comprehensive Guide* 1979 Addison-Wesley Publishing Company; Reading, MA pp10-12

Arthritis pain gives us valuable clues as to the condition of our joints and the progress of our disease. It is not advisable to try to eliminate all pain. But when we already know there's a problem, we'd just as soon have the twinges let up a bit. For this, there are natural chemicals produced in the brain, called endorphins. They act as opiates, attaching themselves to the pain receptor sites and shielding them from pain.

This is where exercise comes in. The much discussed euphoria that comes to runners after they have passed a certain pain level, comes about because the endorphins swing into action. This indicates to some researchers that the exercise itself stimulates the endorphins to do their job. Studies are being conducted to see if there are ways of artificially stimulating these chemical reactions. This could also explain the effect of activity in dissipating morning stiffness.

A serendipitous benefit of exercise is hinted at by a test of senior citizens at the University of Utah. The elderly volunteers, who had slipped into a sedentary way of life, agreed to take up a brisk aerobic conditioning program. A second bunch just put in some time doing simple stretching exercises, and a third kept right on being lazy. The studies, conducted by Dr. Robert Dustman, appear to confirm what we've thought all along, that if you keep active physically, you'll also help keep yourself more alert mentally. After only four months, tests showed significant improvement in memory, reaction time, and mental flexibility in the aerobic group and even, to the researcher's surprise, modest gains for the stretchers. Dustman was quoted in a UPI article as speculating that "those people were so out of shape that even stretching was an improvement." [101]

Type and strenuousness of an exercise program should be dictated by the nature of the patient's associated connective tissue disease, if any. Your doctor may suggest swimming or walking to help maintain flexibility of joints and muscles without placing too much stress on them. There are, according to the Arthritis Foundation's *Arthritis Helpbook*,[102] three basic types of exercise: range of motion, stretching and strengthening, and endurance. The first type is designed to maintain flexibility by moving an individual joint through all of its natural limits in each type of motion it is expected to accomplish. The idea is to go as far as you can comfortably, and then take it just a hair further. Strengthening exercises are done by contracting the muscles without moving the joint (isometric). The isometrics can make you better able to lift and bear weight without harming your inflamed knees or elbows, etc. Endurance exercises, walking, swimming, or even dancing should be done in a smooth stress free style to increase stamina, taking care to avoid damage to the joints. Some sports, while enjoyable as recreation, can be risky. Tennis played on a hard surface can put excessive strains on the knees, hips, and ankles, as well as causing the infamous 'tennis elbow'; bowling with a too-heavy ball can be painful for the elbows and wrists. Here again much depends on the individual. You may be experiencing stiffness in the fingers and find that typing, or even playing computer games, is good exercise. I

---

[101] Robert Dustman "Brisk Walk Aids Mind, Studies Say" UPI Chicago *Houston Post*; 30 Aug 1987

[102] Lorig, *The Arthritis Helpbook*

launched my whole career as a writer because I thought typing might ward off stiffness of the fingers.

Figure 21 Walkin' and Talkin'

Once you start your program it is important to be as regular with it as you can. Often, you will notice that the actual walking can be painful, but this doesn't necessarily mean it's doing any harm. The Arthritis Foundation suggests a rule of thumb: if your exercise causes pain that persists more than two hours after you finish the exercise, you may be putting too much stress on the joint. But don't stop. Just ease up a bit. Walk a shorter distance or a little slower. Or adjust the number of days per week when you walk or swim. But consider that it may take three or four weeks before you feel any appreciable physical benefits. [103] Don't be too quick to get discouraged.

Many areas around the country now have swim exercise programs especially designed for arthritis patients and led by qualified physical therapists. I have found a regular morning walk to be the easiest program to maintain. At first, I walked alone and thought it terribly boring. I found myself making all kinds of excuses to get out of my daily walk. It was too cold out or too hot. Or I had to get the kitchen cleaned. Any excuse was a good excuse. But then I discovered a neighbor who wanted to walk, too. Now we have marked out a route (back and forth down our one block long street a specific number of times to equal the distance goal we have set for ourselves) and we walk and talk five mornings a week. We are flexible enough that obligations that interfere can keep us off a day without stopping the whole procedure. We average four days a week and this seems to bring good results. An added bonus is that we have our own little "group therapy" sessions. We can blow off steam about the frustrations of our lives to each other without having to take out the tensions on family members! We also can share the small triumphs of our lives.

---

[103]Booth "Walking for Arthritis" pp10-12

I am lucky enough to have a hot tub in my home and I find it helpful to exercise each time I take a bath in it. With the wholehearted approval of my doctor, I do bicycle kicks in the water, which I have gradually increased in number over a period of time. I find that a short series of stretching exercises is good to ease the morning stiffness when I first get out of bed.

These are the things that have worked for me. I must emphasize that each person is different and will have a different level of energy and flexibility. Depending on the nature and extent of your arthritic involvement, you may need to work on range of motion exercises for different parts of your body. You must consult with your doctor about which exercises you should do and how strenuous they should be.

Your doctor may recommend a series of physical therapy treatments for you These treatments are discussed in Part 2 Chapter 4,

Relaxation

As with exercise, relaxation technique can provide a measure of cheap, drug free, pain relief. How many of us find ourselves gritting our already abused teeth and tensing our muscles just to get through the challenges of our days! We all know the headaches that come at the end of a long, hard day at the office, especially if the boss has chewed us out over something that wasn't our fault at all. It is not our imagination or just piling one more straw on the camel's back when we find our arthritis acting up at times like these. There is a direct cause and effect here and we can definitely do something about it.

Dianne C. Witter and Pat Hamilton Dickey describe, in *Arthritis Today* [104] special techniques we can learn to unwind those taut muscles and soothe the jangled nerves. To do this we have to be able to recognize the tension, to know in our muscles exactly how it feels, as opposed to the relaxed condition we are hoping to create. For this, psychiatrist Edmund Jacobson devised a practice he calls *progressive relaxation*. Using special exercises, it's possible to tighten individual muscles, hold a few seconds, then release them. In kind of an it-feels-so-good-when-you-stop approach, the pleasant feeling of relaxation that follows can ease the pain of aching joints. And a special plus is that many of the exercises can be done unobtrusively, in your office or anywhere you happen to feel the need. Witter and Dickey do suggest that you first practice them in a restful atmosphere with few distractions until you are able to ignore outside irritations. The specific exercises are detailed in Lorig and Fries' *The Arthritis Helpbook* [105] and reprinted in the *Arthritis Today* article.

Other relaxing ideas include repeating a soothing word or sound to crowd distressing thoughts out of your mind, mentally conjuring up a pleasant time or place that makes you feel at ease; or visualizing a particularly sore joint as hot and inflamed and then mentally picturing it as it cools down, allowing the pain to 'flow' out of it. You can experiment with these techniques to find what works for you and then practice until you can do them easily as needed.

---

[104]Dianne C. Witter and Pat Hamilton Dickey "Relaxation: A Treat of a Treatment for Pain" *Arthritis Today*, October 1987 pp 28-31
[105]Lorig *Arthritis Helpbook*

Other Problem Areas

Dry Skin

Once again the major thrust of therapy for dry skin is to restore the moisture and to try to protect it from further drying out. Bathing should be limited to actual necessity. The Europeans have long derided Americans for taking too many baths. In this case they are right, as strangely enough, soaking in water can draw the moisture out of our already dry skin. Remember as a child the way your finger tips wrinkled up like a prune after a long afternoon in the community swimming pool? This happens in a smaller way each time you wash up. It has to do with osmosis, a condition in which the more highly concentrated of two solutions will pass through a membrane to dilute the weaker solution, in an attempt to create equality. That is, the fluid in your body is the stronger solution and the water in the sink or pool is weaker. So the body fluid seeps out through your skin into the water.

Every time you bathe (and hot tubs or soaking baths can surely feel good on those aching joints!), use as little soap as possible and slather down afterwards with a good moisturizing lotion. Use the lotion before you dry off, so that it will trap the moisture on your skin.

Sunbathing for that glorious tan should be left to others who haven't read or don't believe all the warnings of the harm it can do to even the healthiest skin. What looks lovely on an eighteen-year-old can make a 40 year old look like a senior citizen. Let's get back to the Victorian ideal of soft, unweathered skin as the ultimate beauty.

CREAMS AND LOTIONS
readily available at your favorite drug or department store

Products marked with * are available with SPF 15 sunscreen

Aquaderm	Lubriderm
Almay Moisture Balance*	Moisturel
Alpha Hydrox	Neutragena*
Clinique Turnaround*	Nivea Visage*
Crisco —Yes, the ordinary shortening, believe it or not!)	Nutraderm
Curel	Nutraplus Cream
Dermatology Formula	Oil of Olay*
Eucerin	Ponds*
Keri Lotion	Soft Sense
Lacticare	Soft Skin by Care-Tech
Lancone*	Wondra

Figure 22 Moisturizers

Avoid the sun when possible. Cover up with long sleeves when it's not. Or if you must get right out in it, start slathering again. This time use a good sunscreen, preferably with at least a 15 rating and an added moisturizer for thorough protection.

For convenient one-step coating, try using one of those creams shown in Figure 22 that have SPF 15 UV protection built right in. Dermatologists suggest SPF 15 provides adequate protection for most of us. Lupus patients may want to use higher levels.

The Digestive System

A distressing part of this whole mess can be the digestive upsets that seem to be our constant companions. Beginning with the need to avoid certain foods and having to explain that "it's not that I don't *like* Mexican food, it's just that it doesn't like *me!*" and running the gamut of burps and mysterious pains, we have a lot to contend with in this area. There are some ways to ease it. The most obvious is to limit or avoid foods that you know cause an upset.

Acid foods such as citrus fruits or tomatoes may be the villains. Or highly spiced foods. Chinese food, which I love, seems to give me a lot of trouble. Some people cannot digest milk properly (lactose intolerance) and should be careful of dairy products. Even if the cause of the distress related to a certain food cannot be tied to SS, it still adds to the total level of discomfort. Naturally, you should consider the important elements these foods contain (such as calcium, vitamins, and proteins) and find other sources for them.

Antacids with anti-gas ingredients or acid-inhibiting drugs may be prescribed by your doctor, but should be used only under his supervision. It's only logical that antacids are useless against part of the indigestion of Sjögren's syndrome that is originally caused by a *lack* of acid. This is what happens when SS causes the hydrochloric acid-producing glands to atrophy (literally dry up and fail to secrete enough acid). Similarly, inflammation of the stomach lining itself is not soothed by antacids. In other patients, the heartburn may be brought on by *excess* acid as a result of decreased dilution by saliva. In this case, water alone may bring welcome relief. If refluxing (rising of stomach contents into esophagus) is a problem, it helps to sleep with head elevated. An electric, hospital-style bed where you can raise head and foot to the desired level is ideal if it fits into your budget, but just putting something under the head of your mattress to raise it about 4 inches will achieve the purpose. A few old books you are tired of having around will do.

Cut out those heavy bedtime snacks and turn down burp-producing goodies like onions or baked beans. As a matter of fact, simply remembering not to overeat at any one time will make a difference. But be sure to discuss your digestive problems with your doctor and follow his advice.

The malabsorption (eliac disease,) discussed in Chapter 2, is related to gluten, a protein found in wheat, rye, oats, or barley. Avoiding eating those grains can help.[106] Gluten is hidden in a lot of foods, such as sauces and gravies, so it is important to learn how to distinguish these foods. [107]

For pancreatitis, bed rest is prescribed with intravenous fluids, antibiotics, and sometimes enzyme replacement and antacids[108].

Vaginal Dryness

In Chapter 2, I promised help for this personal aspect of Sjögren's syndrome. As with all the other symptoms, there is no quick and easy solution. But there are ways to ease the discomfort and avoid the more serious consequences. We have seen that dryness can come from

---

[106]Fred F. Pittman and Donald A. Holub "Sjogren's Syndrome and Adult Celiac Disease" Gastroenterology Vol.18, No. 6 1985 pp869-876
[107]Tabor's Cyclopedic Medical Dictionary, Edition 15
[108]David Eiskreis The Gastro-intestinal Tract and Sjögren's Syndrome" BSSA News Vol. 7, No.2

a lot of different causes. Infections, allergies, irritating chemicals, stress, some surgeries, menopause, childbirth, and even hurried sex can be suspected. [109]Allergies and chemicals—including soap, perfumed douches or bubble baths, perspiration, detergents, bath powder, fabric softeners, synthetic fabrics themselves, and even plain tap water (filled with minerals)—can be the most common villains. But they are the most easily remedied. Just say no. To all of those things, you ask? That may not be necessary. Here there is a principal of mechanical trouble shooting that applies. To find out what in particular is bothering you, eliminate one thing at a time. Try just soaking in water with about a tablespoon of vinegar instead of using soap. Use unscented powders. Wear all cotton panties for a while. Experiment with different brands of laundry detergent. One at a time. Then, if the irritation eases, you will know precisely what was causing it. Or if none of those things are guilty, press on to other aspects. Just do some detective work. Are you over tired? Worried about your job? Just feeling irritated at the world? All of these things can slow down the vaginal secretions and leave you dry and uncomfortable. If none of these are the culprit, you will need to work with your doctor, first checking through all the medications you are taking to see if any of them are making you dry. They could be the same ones that affect other parts of your body. He may suggest some changes or he may advise using lubricants. Dr. Thomas Sheehy suggests avoiding Vaseline. Petroleum based products are not biodegradable and their remnants may remain in your body indefinitely. He recommends Lubrin, cold cream and sex, not necessarily in that order.

---

[109] Sheehy *Gynecological Problems*

The latter, he says is "not only beneficial psychologically, but can help restore vaginal lubrication and elasticity, preventing loss of support of the bladder." He adds that when having sex, that pleasurable foreplay serves a definite purpose. Without it the glands may not be properly stimulated to provide lubrication. And that, in turn, can make sexual fulfillment iffy. That's when you need to ask for the loving co-operation of your partner.

Menopause and childbirth related discomfort may be due to a hormone imbalance and this can be checked. When your doctor takes a Pap smear, he can also arrange to test your estrogen level, and if needed, you can take tablets to raise your level. This must be done cautiously and your doctor will probably also prescribe progesterone to ward off the danger of cancer of the uterus. If the Bartholin's glands themselves are the root of the trouble, your gynecologist can unplug them.

A Word to the Wise

On one trip to my doctor's office I happened to wear a lovely copper bracelet my husband had brought me as a souvenir from a trip west. My doctor was upset, until I hastily assured him I expected no magical cures from the bangle. The copper-bracelet-as-arthritis-cure gimmick is relatively innocent, and, in fact, it can be fun to adopt a tongue-in-cheek "let's cover all the bases" approach once in a while. However, there are, and have been as long as people have had "the rheumatiz", shady entrepreneurs who will peddle anything a gullible public will buy as a sure-fire cure for all your aches and pains. Dr. James F. Fries reports, in *Arthritis: A*

Comprehensive Guide, [110] that arthritis patients spend hundreds of millions of dollars per year chasing the rainbows of quick cures. My bracelet was inexpensive and had its own beauty and intrinsic value, but the villains of this story are the predators who will charge just as much as their victims are willing to pay for the wonderful promise of relief. The spectrum ranges from books that promote a quirky diet to "cleanse your system" to elaborate clinics that propose to cure a marvelous variety of ills with a "scientific" new treatment or drug. Large numbers of people travel across the border to Mexico or to other foreign countries to take "miracle" pills which our admittedly cumbersome FDA process prohibits in the US. Among the exotic cures discussed by Dr. Fries are bee sting venom, flu shots, cod liver oil, acupuncture, acupressure, and frequent enemas. The cod liver oil is used to "oil" the joints! Acupuncture, whatever benefits it may have, has been shown to have no effect on arthritis and is not used for that purpose even in China. Those prohibited pills are either being tested to prove their safety and efficacy, or have already been proven to lack those qualities. In spite of glorious claims, for instance, the industrial solvent DMSO has not been proven effective for arthritis, although it is approved for urologists to use as a treatment for interstitial cystitis. The legal pain pills advertised ubiquitously on our TV as being specially formulated for arthritis, are no better than the plain varieties of aspirin, only more expensive.

The wonderful world of quackery has thrived through the ages. Probably as long as there have been human ailments. The record of those ailments goes

---

[110]Fries *Arthritis*

back a long way. In 1856 a well preserved spine from a Neanderthal man was found, cruelly distorted by arthritis. Eric Jameson records, in his *The Natural History of Quackery* [111] a story originally published in the *Northern Imposter* in 1786 of "the Late, Celebrated, Dr. Rock", as follows:

> He was standing one day at his door on Ludgate Hill, when a real doctor of Physic passed, who had learning and abilities, but whose modesty was the true cause of his poverty.
>
> "How comes it," says he to the quack, "that you without education, without skill, without the least knowledge of science, are enabled to live in the style you do? You keep your town house, your carriage, and your country house: whilst I, allowed to possess some knowledge, have neither, and can hardly pick up a subsistence!"
>
> "Why look ye," said Rock smiling, "how many people do you think have passed since you asked me the question?"
>
> "Why," answered the Doctor, "perhaps a hundred."
>
> "And how many out of those hundred, think you, possess common sense?"
>
> "Possibly one," answered the Doctor.
>
> "Then," said Rock, "that one comes to you: and I take care of the other ninety-nine."

Jameson records the story of another physician, working a hundred years earlier, named Paracelsus, who

---

[111] Eric Jameson *The Natural History of Quackery* 1961 Springfield IL Charles C Thomas Publishers

proposed an ingenious cure for disease. His treatment involved a magnet impregnated with "mummy," preferably one made from a criminal who had been hanged, as from these there was a "gentle siccation that expungeth the watery humor". After sowing some "seeds that have a congruity with the disease," the practitioner was to rub the "mummified" magnet over the affected parts of the patient and plunge it into the earth near the planted seeds. As the seeds germinated and grew, the disease would be drawn out of the patient and he would be cured. "Forget the old classical medicine," Paracelsus told his students, "and follow my doctrines."

By the year that twisted old cave man was found, living Americans with the same painful problem had an astounding 1500 different nostrums to choose from. Most were blends of alcohol, narcotics, or a variety of toxic substances added to flavored sugar water. Even today, according to the Consumer's Union's *Report on Fake Health Claims, Worthless Remedies, and Unproven Therapies*,[112] 32 million arthritic Americans spend 950 million a year on their quest for relief. You may say, so what? If I have the money, why not try anything just in case? Even a mummified magnet, if there's any chance at all? Well, of course, the first answer to that is safety. Some of those non-legal cures can actually be harmful, particularly fad diets that neglect vital nutritional needs. Some medications can seriously affect other body systems, or are just plain toxic., especially under uncontrolled circumstances. But Dr. Fries points out that most quack treatments are not actually harmful or

---

[112]Editors of Consumer Reports Books *Consumer's'Union'sReport on Fake Health Claims, Worthless Remedies, and Unproved Therapies,*1980 Consumer's Union Mt Vernon NY

they wouldn't last long. After all, we may have creaky joints but we are not dumb. If people are being harmed, most of us eventually find out and quit buying that one.

So if they won't hurt us, maybe they *will* help. It's worth a try, we say. But if they are not harmful medically, they can have other unpleasant consequences. Some people who try these treatments, turn their backs on the traditional methods their doctors are using. Thus they are not getting the best treatment that our medical knowledge provides for them. The disease may be progressing in a direction that could have been prevented. And when the phony cures don't work, we become discouraged with all treatment, losing confidence and the will to carry on.

Obviously not a satisfactory situation. Of course, having to say our disease is chronic and incurable is not satisfactory either. I don't like that any more than you do. But facing that and doing what we can within that (temporary, we hope) limitation is far better than wasting our resources chasing those slippery rainbows. Besides, we then have the extra satisfaction of knowing that those sleazy con-men cannot succeed, if we don't buy.

None of this applies to the legitimate efforts of dedicated scientists to find the solutions for us. Some of these stories will be told in the chapter on research, and may, truthfully, seem much more exciting than even the most exotic of the snake oil merchants' claims!

Chapter 7 - Research

Letters from readers of *Sjögren's Syndrome: The Sneaky "Arthritis"* are still coming in with the same question; "Are they doing some research about this disease?" And the answer is still, "Yes, they definitely are, even more." Eminent doctors and scientists literally around the world are working diligently to pry open the secrets of cause and effect that create Sjögren's syndrome. That has not always been true. For many years, as many of us are well aware, SS was an orphan disease, hardly even earning recognition as a *disease*, but just considered a rare combination of annoying symptoms. But in recent decades, and particularly in the eighties and nineties, the quest has finally taken hold. Specialists around the world in almost every discipline that enters into the Sjögren's puzzle are conducting experiments and following lines of study about the causes, course, and treatment of SS.

Chronology

While dedicated doctors such as Dr. Norman Talal, who works through the Division of Clinical Immunology and Arthritis at the University of Texas Health Science Center in San Antonio, Texas, have been concerned with these studies for several decades, publishing findings on lymphoma in SS as early as 1963, and Martin Shearn, then an Associate Professor of Medicine at the University of California at San Francisco, wrote his book, *Sjögren's Syndrome* in 1971, the real momentum picked up in the eighties. Drs. N. A. Pavlidis, Karsh, and Moutsopoulos suggested designations of primary and secondary Sjögren's syndrome in 1981, based on studies showing clinical, serological and immunologic differences between SS alone and SS with an associated connective tissue disease[113] Drs. Prause, of Copenhagen, Manthorpe of Sweden's Lund University, Frost-Larsen, and Isager also favored the introduction of the terms primary and secondary.[114]

In May, 1986, Prause joined with Manthorpe to host the 1st International Seminar on Sjögren's Syndrome in Copenhagen. Researchers gathered from countries as far separated as the United States, Greece and Japan to present the findings of their individual investigations. A major achievement of the conference was the discussion of the varied diagnostic criteria then in use and efforts to come to a consensus for worldwide standardization of these criteria.

In October of 1988, Talal hosted the 2nd International Sjögren's Syndrome Symposium at Austin, Texas. Ninety-seven researchers from 14 countries reported on their findings in the areas of immunology and clinical studies in internal medicine, ophthalmology, and oral medicine. There was considerable discussion of the role, if any, of Epstein-Barr virus (EBV) in the development of SS and an as yet unidentified retrovirus was suggested as a possible cause. Once more the subject of criteria was explored, but without a firm

---

[113]Moutsopoulos*Differences in Clinical Manifestations of Sicca Syndrome*
[114]Rolf Manthorpe et al "Editorial Comments to the Four Sets of Criteria for Sjögren's Syndrome". *Scandinavian Journal of Rheumatology;* 1986; Suppl. 61: pp31-35

conclusion. The conference ended with plans for a third meeting in Greece and the hope that definite progress towards cause and cure would be made in the meantime.[115]

At the 3rd International SS Symposium in Ioannina, Greece, in June of 1991, 108 papers were presented under the leadership of Dr. H. M. Moutsopoulos of the University of Ioannina Medical School. Subjects covered at this time included studies of the eyes in SS, the mouth and dental problems, cellular and immunologic studies probing for the cause of SS in genetic, and viral studies and a variety of treatment proposals.

Diagnostic techniques such as labial biopsies, scanning microscopy, impression cytology, and scintigraphy were studied. The discussion of EBV as a cause of SS was continued with some positive and some negative conclusions. Several reports were made indicating that a retrovirus similar to, but not the same as, the HIV virus may be involved in SS. One international study, a comparison of autoantibody responses in Caucasian, Chinese, and Japanese patients by the Scripps Clinic's Dr. Robert Fox and colleagues in the United States, China, and Japan, grew out of information exchanged at the 2nd symposium and was presented at the 3rd symposium.[116]

For the first time, at the Greek conference, a segment was set aside for patient advocate organizations such as the National Sjögren's Syndrome Association and the Sjögren's Syndrome Foundation of the United

[115]Norman Talal, Ed. *Sjögren's Syndrome: A Model for Understanding Autoimmunity* London Academic Press 1989 pp1-2

[116]Abstracts from Third International Symposium on Sjögren's Syndrome; *Clinical and Experimental Rheumatology* 9/3 May-June 1991pp311-340

States to report on their activities to increase the knowledge of SS and to provide support for patients. A Greek patient leader spoke of the need of such an organization in her country.

The 4th SS Symposium was scheduled for August 1993 in Tokyo, Japan under the leadership of Dr. Mitsuo Homma. The tradition has now been well established that the leading members of the SS research community meet periodically to exchange information on the results of their many and varied studies into all aspects of SS. These meetings provide an atmosphere of intellectual and social interchange (a good time is had by all and, as a side effect, international understanding is increased) that can be of enormous benefit to all SS patients. The aggregate of their learning is pooled and, as Talal said in his report on the 2nd symposium, "hopefully cross-fertilized in such a way that the sum would be greater than its individual parts."

The two years between conferences were productive ones, and the symposium has grown not only in size but in depth of the information presented. 118 participants presented 41 papers and 125 poster presentations in Tokyo. Topics covered ocular and oral studies, criteria, clinical, immunological, histological and molecular research, with sessions on autoantibodies, viral factors, and lymphoproliferative disorders. Clinical studies addressed causes, effects, and treatments.[117]

The process of sharing information across national borders and medical disciplines continues. The Japanese hosts presented a superbly organized and elegant meeting. Dr. Aike A. Kruize of the Netherlands announced

---

[117] *IVth International Symposium on Sjögren's Syndrome: Program - Abstracts* Tokyo, Japan 1993

that the 5th Symposium would be held in June 1995 in Amsterdam.

Causes Under Study

Viral Possibilities

As early as the 1988 symposium, three scientists reported their suspicion of a connection between the Epstein-Barr virus and Sjögren's Syndrome. The consensus then seemed to be that the virus probably didn't cause the disease but might play a part in its development.[118] By the time of the 1991 conference, a growing number of investigators suggested a strong involvement of EBV in the course of SS. Drs. Cecelia. A. Crouse at the University of Miami School of Medicine, Mutsuto Tateishi and Kasuo Tsubota of the Tokyo Medical and Dental University and Zhang Naizheng of the Peking Union Medical College presented papers on EBV. While its role in the disease process has not been pinpointed, there are continuing studies following up the demonstrated possibilities.

Crouse and her colleagues found latent EBV in normal lacrimal glands in 1990 and suggested this could be a site of infection if the virus were reactivated.[119]

Drs. Robert Fox and Ho-Il Kang of Scripps Clinic, suggest, in a 1992 report, that since EBV is a strong stimulator of T cell responses, a vicious circle of cause

[118]*Sjögren's Syndrome: A Model for Understanding Autoimmunity* Ed. NormanTalal Academic Press San Diego 1989 p1

[119]Cecelia A. Crouse et al, "Detection of Epstein-Barr Virus Genomes in Normal Human Lacrimal Glands" *Journal of Clinical Microbiology,* May 1990 pp1026-1032

and effect[120] may exist if T cells are also a factor in the EBV re-activation.

Dr. Stephen Pflugfelder, at University of Miami, reported in 1993, finding EBV in the lacrimal glands of a significantly greater number of Sjögren's syndrome patients than those of patients without Sjögren's syndrome.[121] The non SS patients had many of the type of T cells known as CD8 which specifically attack the Epstein Barr B virus. But there are two types of EBV and these cells are effective only against one type. They reduce the fever of a B cell infected with EBV type 1 but not with EBV type 2. Pflugfelder and his colleagues found only type 2 EBV surviving in the normal lacrimal glands. By contrast, the Sjögren's patients, whose glands contain CD4 T cells, rather than CD8, had surviving EBV type 1. It is possible that the SS patients lack the ability to kill off the type 1 strain of EBV. If so, treatment might be aimed at encouraging the immune system to attack the type 1 virus to prevent or even possibly undo the destruction of the glands.[122]

Dr. C. Baboonian and his colleagues wrote of finding anti-herpes virus 6 antibodies in 90% of their patients in 1990.[123]

Also in 1990, Dr. Robert F. Garry of Tulane University in New Orleans, LA, reported the detection of a previously unknown retrovirus derived from two

[120]Robert Fox and Ho-il Kang "Pathogenisis of Sjogren's Syndrome" *Rheumatic Disease Clinics of America: Sjogren's Syndrome* W, B, Saunders Company, Philadelphia 1992 p 532

[121]Stephen C. Pflugfelder et al "Amplification of Epstein-Barr virus genomic sequences in blood cells, lacrimal glands, and tears from primary Sjögren's Syndrome patients" *Ophthalmology* 1990; 97:pp976-984

[122]Pflugfelder, "Epstein-Barr Virus and the Lacrimal Gland Pathology of Sjögren's Syndrome" In press.

[123]C. Baboonian et al "Antibodies to human herpes virus in Sjögren's Syndrome" *Arthritis Rheum* 1990 33: pp1749-1750

Sjögren's syndrome patients. The new retrovirus was named human intracisternal A-type retroviral particle (HIAP). Further tests found that antibodies to HIAP appeared in many Sjögren's syndrome patients, indicating an unproven possibility that it could be related to the disease. HIAP is not contagious. When this news was widely reported in newspapers, some people, aware that AIDS is also caused by a retrovirus, were concerned. Although scientists have observed "Sjögren's syndrome-like" symptoms in AIDS patients, there is no need for concern. HIV differs dramatically from HIAP in structure and function. It is possible that the new retrovirus causes immune disease by mimicking host tissues. Normally the host would not make antibodies to these proteins, but if it does, these antibodies might not be able to distinguish between the invading retrovirus and the normal tissue it mimics.[124] Several studies were presented at the Ioannina Symposium in 1991.[125]

The jury is still out on the role of viruses in SS, but there are ongoing studies searching for the answer. The current consensus seems to be that one or more of these viruses *may* be cause or causes of SS, or at least affect its progress.

Dr. Robert Fox suggested three possibilities for the involvement of viruses in the cause of SS. One, it may be that several viruses can trigger the syndrome. Secondly, the primary cause could be a virus not yet identified and those known may be secondary to it. A third suggestion is that the viruses do not cause SS but

[124]Robert F. Garry "Detection of a Human Intracisternal A-Type Retroviral Particle Antigenically Related to HIV" *Science* 250, pp1127-1129, 1990

[125]"Third International Symposium on Sjögren's Syndrome - Abstracts" Eds. H. M. Moutsopoulos et al *Clinical and Experimental Rheumatology* vol 9 - #3 May/June 1991pp336337

merely influence its progression and symptoms. The viruses being considered include the Epstein-Barr virus, Herpes 6, Hepatitis B or C, retroviruses, other viruses whose structure is similar to SS autoantigens or a gene that resembles a retrovirus reactivated in SS.[116]

Hormonal and Other Factors

Talal's group, having noted the predominance of women among SS patients, looked for the influence of sex hormones. Their findings showed that estrogen encouraged the development of autoantibodies in laboratory mice, while androgens tended to suppress them. Talal reported at the International Conference on the Lacrimal Gland in Bermuda in 1992, that a particular type of B cell, which is found in newborn babies but normally dies off, is found to increase instead in SS patients.[126] These and certain persistent genetic elements may be basic to SS.

In conjunction with the Audie Murphy Memorial Veterans Hospital and Medical Center Hospital, the Division of Clinical Immunology of the University of Texas Health Science Center maintains an NIH-funded Multipurpose Arthritis Center. Within this organization there is a special multidisciplinary clinic devoted to patients with Sjögren's syndrome. In relation to immunology and autoimmunity; their special research interests include, causes and effects, cell biology, lymphocytic abnormalities, nutrition, sex hormone

[126]Norman Talal, "Sjögren's Syndrome (SS): Close To Cause and Cure?" *International Conference on the Lacrimal Gland, Tear Film and Dry Eye Syndrome: Basic Science and Clinical Relevance* at Bermuda; Program and Abstract Book 1992. p 129

modulation, rheumatic disease, and epidemiology. The clinics see as many as 5000 patients a year.[127] Talal is particularly interested in discovering the cause and development of autoimmune diseases and has done studies of the relationship of retroviral involvement in SS. Talal and his colleagues at San Antonio are studying T cells, cytokines, the activation of lymphocytes, and the relationship of such factors as nutrition, aging, and sex hormones to the immune responses. Similar study programs are being carried out at other centers both in the United States and in other countries around the world.

Dr. Austin Mircheff and his colleagues at the University of Southern California School of Medicine have studied the mechanism of tear production. They describe the lacrimal glands as bundles of small tubes blending into ducts to carry fluid to the surface of the eye. Each begins as a hollow bulb made of a single layer of cells. An enzyme (called Na+,K+-ATPase) pumps electric particles back and forth through the cell layer in a kind of recycling traffic pattern that also uses transport proteins. In their study, they were surprised to discover a large number of these pumps and transport proteins in membranes inside the cells. These create a reserve supply of tears to be released by neurotransmitters (nerve messengers from the brain) for which they found abundant receptors.[128] After determining that females have proportionately more of the pumps, the scientists studied the effects of estrogen

[127] U Texas Health Science Center. Rheumatology/ClinicalImmunology Fellowship Training Brochure 1987

[128] Austin Mircheff, "Understanding the Causes of Lacrimal Insufficiency: Implications for Treatment and Prevention of Dry Eye Syndrome" Presented to the Science Writers Seminar in Ophthalmology, Research to Prevent Blindness; Universal City, CA Apr 25-28, 1993 pp2-9

and androgen hormones on the lacrimal (tear) glands and concluded specific levels of both hormones are needed to maintain a proper supply of tears. Strangely, high levels of estrogen (as in pregnancy) and low levels (after menopause) both go along with dry eyes. This they explain because androgens are in short supply in both cases. Mircheff's team and others are continuing to research the possibility that androgen replacement therapy may keep the glands functioning when natural supplies are low, and may even restore damaged glands. Androgen replacement therapy may also be a way to reduce new cases of SS. Dr. David Sullivan of Harvard Medical School, has already used testosterone (an androgen) to dramatically decrease the number of lymphocytes in tear gland tissue of mice. [129]

Sullivan suggests that in SS, the secretion of tears may be weakened by hormonal imbalance . He lists other possible causes for the short supply of tears as; destruction of tear-producing cells in the glands by T cells, interference with stimulation of the glands by an excess of cytokines, damage of cell membranes by overactive genes, or lymphocytic infiltration which may simply squeeze the ducts closed. [116]

Dr. John Tiffany of Oxford University reported on the composition and structure of the tear film at the Lacrimal Gland conference in Bermuda in November of 1992. He discussed the extreme difficulty in measuring the various components of tears. The principle of physics that says that what ever you observe will be changed by the fact that you are observing it applies here. Most methods of gathering tears from a

---

[129]David Sullivan et al, Androgen induced Suppression of Autoimmune Disease in Lacrimal Glands of Mouse Models of Sjögren's Syndrome" *International Conference on the Lacrimal Gland, Tear* ...Bermuda, 1992. p 125

living eye, can materially affect the tears. Tiffany questions the established theory that the mucus layer of tears is necessary for the stability of the tear film that protects the cornea. He also notes findings that the mucus layer is thicker than has been estimated. He suggests that the knowledge about tear film is far from complete and that there are "a very large number of avenues open for study."

A new interest was shown at the Tokyo conference in studying the presence of cytokines in salivary gland tissue. These specifically include interleukin (IL), tumor necrosis factor (TNF), interferon (IFN), and transforming growth factor (TGF). Cytokine is defined[130] as a "generic term for non-antibody proteins released by one cell population on contact with specific antigens which act as intracellular mediators as in generation of an immune response." That is, though not actually antibodies, they act as if they were. The researchers have noted that certain cytokines are present in the salivary gland tissue of SS patients and others are either absent or weak. This could indicate that these proteins either cause or control the inflammation of SS.[116] Further studies along this line may provide new treatment possibilities.

Treatments

Dr. Philip Fox's work at the National Institute of Dental Research, NIH in Bethesda, Maryland, focuses on ways to relieve and treat the oral components of SS. A 1991 study report by Fox, Jane Atkinson and

---

[130] Dorland's Medical Dictionary

colleagues[131] concludes that pilocarpine relieved complaints of oral dryness in almost 90% of the participants. It appeared to have only mild side effects and to be helpful in stimulating saliva output where there was still some remaining function of the glands. Dr. Nelson Rhodus has also studied pilocarpine at the University of Minneapolis, arriving at a similar conclusion.[132] Pilocarpine is also presently used as an ingredient in some prescription eye drops.[133]

Dr. E. Johannes 's-Gravenmade and Arjan Vissink of the University of Groningen in the Netherlands have tested a mucin-containing lozenge which works well as a time release method of moistening the mouth. They have suggested this as a possible delivery system for pilocarpine and as an infection preventive.[134]

There appears to be a long standing precedent for the use of pilocarpine. It was the basis of a treatment, tincture of Jaborandi, reported in 1888 by Dr. Hadden for a patient who had a severe dry mouth. The South American plant was first used as a medicine in 1874 by Dr. Coutinhou of Pernambuco. Imported in England, it was named *pilocarpus jaborandi* in 1893.

The NIDR team also conducted studies to find ways to measure normal and abnormal swallowing abilities, especially among SS patients.[135]

[131]Philip Fox, et al "Pilocarpine Treatment of Salivary Gland Hypofunction and Dry Mouth (Xerostomia)" *Archives of Internal Medicine* Vol 151, June 1991 pp1149-1152

[132]Nelson Rhodus "Effects of Pilocarpine on Salivary Flow in Patients with Sjögren's Syndrome" *Oral Surgery* 1991 Nov; 72 (5):545-9

[133]NIDR *Dry Mouth*

[134]E. Johannes 's-Gravenmade and Arjan Vissink "Mucin-containing lozenges in the treatment of intraoral problems associated with Sjögren's Syndrome" *Oral Surgery Oral Medicine Oral Pathology* April 1993 pp466-471

[135]Anthony J. Caruso et al "Objective Measures of Swallowing in Patients with Primary Sjögren's Syndrome" *Dysphagia* 4: 101-105 1989

Dr. Troy Daniels, a dentist at the University of California-San Francisco Sjögren's Syndrome Clinic, is especially interested in studying the immune system diseases of the mouth and salivary glands.[136]At the clinic, under Dr. Daniels and Dr. Ostler, with Dr. John P. Whitcher, patients are referred by dentists, ophthalmologists and rheumatologists for diagnosis and management.[137]

Dr. Frank C. Arnett, Dir. of Rheumatology Div., University of Texas Health Science Center - Houston, is studying the incidence of neonatal lupus with mothers carrying the anti-Ro (SS-A) antibody, a Sjögren's syndrome marker.

Arnett, and his colleague, Dr. John D. Reveille, have published studies[138] noting a frequent association of Sjögren's syndrome with other autoimmune diseases and autoantibodies in different members of a family. This, they conclude, suggests a genetic influence in the cause of SS.

At the Rheumatology and Clinical Immunology Divisions of the Department of Medicine of Johns Hopkins University in Baltimore, Maryland, Dr. Elaine Alexander is currently investigating the effects of SS on central (CNS, brain and spinal cord) and peripheral (PNS, all other parts) nervous system disorders. Although scientists generally recognize that such peripheral effects as trigeminal nerve problems and burning sensations can be Sjögren's-related, the area of

[136]Troy Daniels et al Sjögren's Syndrome Clinic, University of CA/San Francisco; May 1985

[137]Troy Daniels et al Sjögren's Syndrome Clinic, University of CA/San Francisco; May 1985

[138]John D. Reveille and Frank C. Arnett "The Immunogenetics of Sjögren's Syndrome" Rheumatic Disease Clinics of North America: Sjögren's Syndrome Vol. 18, Number 3 W. B. Saunders Company, Philadelphia,August 1992 pp539-549

CNS-SS (SS-related central nervous system disorders) remains controversial. Alexander first described cases from her clinic in 1981 and has continued to accumulate evidence to support her position. Other researchers have devoted studies to proving or disproving a connection with mixed results. They have often dismissed her results as being based on a weighted population; that is, most of her patients come to her because they have some sort of CNS problems and therefore her statistics are not typical of the general SS population. She freely admits that her SS patients are "highly selected"[139] (20% to 25% of them have CNS disease) but notes that her estimates are similar to numbers reported by Finnish researcher Hietaharju.[140].

Alexander has used magnetic resonance imaging (MRI) to pinpoint areas of the brain that show inflammation (excess lymphocytes.) She has also used electrophysiologic studies and cerebrospinal fluid analysis as diagnostic procedures. These tests have indicated that patients may have a wide range of problems including speech difficulties, recent memory loss, and bladder or motor nerve involvement. The list is extensive and can be worrisome, but the good news is that Alexander considers these symptoms to be "potentially treatable and reversible." She has found that patients respond to corticosteroid therapy. For this reason she recommends that SS patients with indications of CNS involvement be thoroughly evaluated to decide on a treatment plan.

---

[139]Elaine Alexander, "Central Nervous System Disease in Sjögren's Syndrome" *Rheumatic Disease Clinics of America: Sjögren's Syndrome* pp637-672
[140]A. Hietaharju

Japanese interest in SS began with a report made by Dr. K. Okajima in 1938[141], but it wasn't until the late 70s that concern spread from the ophthalmologists to include researchers in rheumatology and immunology. Official studies were conducted from 1976 to 1980 by an SS research committee, headed by Dr. Tadashi Ofuji, (president of Okayama University in 1987) with Dr. Shoji Miyawaki of the University's 3rd Department of Internal Medicine, and sponsored by the Japanese Health and Welfare Ministry.

More recently, Dr. Susumu Sugai, at Kanazawa Medical University in Ishikawa, Japan has been studying the reasons B cells begin to rapidly reproduce themselves in some SS patients, with an eye to deciding on appropriate treatments for these patients. Drs. Kasuo Tsubota and Ichiro Saito and colleagues in Tokyo have concerned themselves with methods of diagnosis and treatment in addition to immunologic studies. They have described refinements to the Schirmer test and special sensors to measure tear evaporation. Special glasses have been designed to provide extra moisture around the eyes.

In a different direction, the Japanese scientists are also investigating the traditional system of Kampo medicines, "herbal remedies" which are being used in combination with western techniques by many practicing doctors. Kampo medicine is based on observance of the patient's symptoms and adjusting treatment as necessary (in the experience of many SS patients, that doesn't sound so different!) while the western approach is usually to find the cause and try to eliminate it. Since

---

[141]K. Okajima "Ceratoconjunctivitis sicca" (in Japanese) Ganka Rinshou 33: 1079, 1938

many of the drugs have been in use in Japan beginning between the third and eighth centuries, it is obviously possible that they will hold up under western style scrutiny. Early studies have been done on ginseng for circulatory disorders and glycyrrhizin for chronic hepatitis. Drugs called Bakumondo-to, Byakko-ka-ninjinton, and Juzendaihotō were mentioned at Tokyo as being helpful for KCS and dry mouth.

Dr. Prause, at Denmark's University of Copenhagen, began studying Sjögren's syndrome in 1972. Beginning with a small group of scientists who were personal friends, the research effort grew to include investigators from other parts of Denmark, from Sweden and from Norway to evolve into an all-Scandinavia Sjögren's group. They established a journal to standardize the way they report their medical findings and then carried that idea even further into the contemporary world of medical research. They began compiling patient data and are currently working to set up a centralized computer database. It will contain the medical information gained from SS patients throughout the Scandinavian countries, which will be very useful in creating wide based studies in many aspects of Sjögren's syndrome with the shortest possible time required to accumulate large amounts of information. This will allow the same sets of tests to be used in many studies, creating an exchange of knowledge, and avoiding the duplication of effort while at the same time putting the available research dollars to maximum use.

In Greece, studies by Dr. H. M. Moutsopoulos, Dr. Stavros H. Constantopoulos, and their colleagues in the Department of Internal Medicine at the University of Ioannina's Medical School have investigated the areas of lung disease and kidney and gastrointestinal problems in Sjögren's syndrome. Aspects of salivary gland involvement have also been studied. Further work in clinical, immunologic, and viral data were presented at the 1991 Symposium in Ioannina by Moutsopoulos' group. Corneal ulcers, impression cytology as a diagnostic technique, anti-microbial antibodies and the possibility of a reactivated virus as a factor in SS were discussed.

Dr. Moutsopoulos worked with SS patients initially in San Francisco and at the United States' National Institutes of Health (1976-1980) and then returned to his native Greece. There his Immunology Laboratory for clinical (diagnostic) and research work follows over 100 patients with primary Sjögren's and many with secondary SS.

Investigators in The Netherlands have given considerable attention (as have others) on standardizing the international criteria for SS studies. They note five distinct systems, adding "Daniels and Talal" to the four (California, Copenhagen, Greece, and Japan) discussed at the Copenhagen Symposium. A. A. Kruize et al conclude that an extended inventory of nervous system and musculoskeletal involvement with immunologic data is essential to further study of SS.[142] The national patient's organization of the Netherlands, Nationale Verenining Sjögren's-patienten, reported on a survey of 520 patients in 1991 listing 22 symptoms, using the Talal/Daniels criteria. A not surprising result showed that a great majority of patients suffered from eye and mouth complaints and fatigue. Skin, vaginal, and in-

---

[142]A. A. Kruize"Neuro-musculo-skeletal manifestations in primary Sjögren's Syndrome" Netherlands Journal of Medicine 40 (1992) 135-139

testinal problems followed in that order. This study was compared with an earlier (1988) survey of 250 patients with almost identical results.

Others are carrying out a wide variety of studies in the People's Republic of China, France and the former Soviet Union.

Arthritis

In the broader field of arthritis research, investigators are taking several different approaches. Immunologists tracking the cellular basis of inflammatory diseases are now carrying their studies on beyond that to the molecular level and are hoping to identify points in the process that may be blockable with new drugs. Researchers are looking for ways to "turn off" the defective genes that trigger autoimmune responses. Dr. Robert Fox and his colleagues at the Research Institute of Scripps Clinic in La Jolla, California, have conducted an extensive variety of studies covering the broad spectrum of SS concerns. Clues are being unearthed to the genetic factors involved which will help doctors anticipate the development of disease. Better knowledge of the mechanics of joint movement and interaction will lead to more understanding of the beneficial exercises and ways to limit damage to bones, and tissues while studies of the chemical structure of cartilage is expected to yield progress in preventive medication in this area. Other researchers are looking for new ways to use existing drugs and procedures such as irradiation and a treatment known as plasmapheresis, which aims at cleansing offending substances from the blood.

Many of these studies, being carried out with special regard to rheumatoid arthritis, lupus, and other autoimmune diseases will have effects on the work on Sjögren's syndrome, and some data gained from SS work will impact the entire field.

More Treatments Being Studied and Some Unproven Remedies

The fact that SS and some of the other autoimmune diseases (particularly lupus) appear most inclined to attack women, and especially women in the childbearing years, inspired researchers to look for a connection. Dr. Talal reported in 1978 on studies that seem to indicate that female sex hormones (estrogen) can exacerbate autoimmune diseases while male hormones (androgens) tend to suppress them. Alfred Steinberg, whose research interest started in Talal's laboratory, and others at the National Institutes of Health (NIH) observed that male hormones tend to favor the suppressor T cells while female hormones encourage the production of helper T cells, which we learned earlier stimulate the activities of both the killer T cells and the antibody-producing B cells.[143] There is some evidence that lupus patients may benefit from androgen treatment (Danazol).[144] Dr. S. Ansar Ahmed is conducting ongoing studies in San Antonio into the control of immunity and autoimmunity by sex hormones.[145]

Bromhexine is a drug that increases bronchial secretions and reduces viscosity. Produced commercially in

---

[143]Mizel *In Self Defense*

[144]Norman Talal "Sex Hormones and Modulation of Immune Response in SLE" Clinics in Rheumatic Diseases April 1982; 8: 23-27

[145]Norman Talal, Ansar Ahmed "Immunomoduulation by Hormones - An Area of Growing Importance" *The Journal of Rheumatology*; 1987; 14: 191-193

Europe as Bisolvon™, bromhexine comes from an old Indian folk herb medicine that has been extracted from the plant, *Adhatoda vasica*, for more than 500 years.[146] Dr. Prause, has studied the use of bromhexine, and it is used routinely in Europe for bronchitis as well as to improve tear and saliva secretions.[147] It has not yet been approved for use in the United States. Positive results have been seen in tests on laboratory mice and, additionally, the drug seems to lessen the destruction of tissue by deranged immune cells. Because of its long history, the drug is not patentable, which puts it into the class of drugs whose lack of profitability makes them impractical for American drug firms to produce. The costs of testing to satisfy the Food and Drug Administration's strict safety and effectiveness standards are high but Boehringer-Ingelheim Pharmaceuticals Inc., a US company was initiating Investigational New Drug studies needed to make the drug legal here.

Drs. Prause and Manthorpe have also conducted placebo studies on another plant derivative drug. A fatty acid (gamma-linolenic acid or GLA) derived from evening primrose oil is being suggested as a means of promoting the body's production of prostaglandins used to fight infection and inflammation.[148] The GLA works by supplying needed chemicals to produce prostaglandin EI, which helps regulate the inflammatory process. Evening primrose oil, which is manufactured as Efamol must be used at least a month for any benefits. The Scandinavian tests indicated that those patients experienced a lessening of the universal

[146]Manthorpe *Criteria for Sjögren's Syndrome*

[147]E. Rooney, H. Lindsley "Sjögren's Syndrome - An Update" The Journal of the Kansas Medical Society; September 1983: 482-485

[148]Manthorpe "Sjögren's Syndrome: Immunological Features"

tiredness that accompanies SS. However, Dr. Frank Arnett of the University of Texas Health Science Center at Houston, describes it as an unproven remedy and does not recommend its use.

In Greece, Dr. Moutsopoulos and his associates have conducted clinical trials of cyclosporin A, another plant-related substance, but the results were disappointing. Although a decrease in destructive lymphocytes was seen, little actual improvement in the patients' condition was observed.[149]

Some studies into the use of Vitamin A in eye drops have been controversial. Although the vitamin is used in Europe, there have been no proven effects when taken internally, and tests of its topical use (directly in the eyes) have all been open studies (without the double blind control in which neither doctor nor patient knows who is getting what treatment). Because people tend to want to have good results, Dr. Prause comments, "These all turn out positive." One such test, carried out in 1984 by Dr. Scheffer Chuei-Goong Tseng then at the Massachusetts Eye and Ear Infirmary of Harvard Medical School, followed the treatment of 22 dry eye patients, some of whom had been diagnosed as having Sjögren's syndrome. All were selected because conventional methods had not helped them, and all reported improvement in tear production and vision and relief from dryness, irritation, and light sensitivity. The treatment utilized an ointment containing Vitamin A.

Dr. Etsuko Takamura of Tokyo Women's Medical College reported at the Tokyo Symposium that topical

149 Alexandros Drosos et al ."Cyclosporin A Therapy in Patients with Primary Sjögren's Syndrome: Results at One Year." *Scandinavian Journal of Rheumatology*; 1986; Suppl. 61: 246-249

applications of Vitamin A supplement were effective in treating the surface of eyes damaged by the lack of tears. In a paper delivered to a Science Writers Seminar in Ophthalmology,[150] Dr. Tseng states that he observed reversal of damaged tissue and regeneration of goblet (mucus-secreting) cells; that "this new method of treatment...appears to be the first, to the best of our knowledge, that can reverse the diseased tissue change."

Fortunately for us as Sjögren's patients, the negative or questionable results of some experiments cannot deter these investigators from pursuing other avenues and new findings are being uncovered a rapid rate. Much new information will have been uncovered even before this book can be completed and with the increased awareness and concern by researchers, health professionals and patients themselves, progress is bound to be made.

---

[150]Scheffer Tseng "Topical Vitamin A Treatment for Dry Eye Disorders" Science Writers Seminar in Ophthalmology Research To Prevent Blindness, Inc. Washington DC: 2 Oct 1984

Chapter 8 - Prognosis

For most patients SS has a benign course; that is, its multiple symptoms provide only varying degrees of inconvenience or discomfort. But that does not mean, as some medical practitioners have felt, that it should be taken lightly. When I recently remarked to my pharmacist that there ought to be a specialty known as exocrinology, he replied that the exocrine glands were not considered very important! You have only to have them fail to function properly to realize how far from the mark that comment is. True, the vast majority of Sjögren's patients never experience any life-threatening difficulties, but the problems can certainly be life*style* threatening. The very fact that a Sjögren's patient quite often shows no visible signs of illness, can cause major misunderstandings among families and coworkers. The need for rest periods when your flag suddenly droops is rarely obvious to companions. A dilemma occurs for the patient who doesn't want to be a complainer and yet has a need for some people close to her to know what is going on for her. I have always had a philosophy that says if you have a problem, (the illness) that's one problem; if you moan and complain about it, you then have two problems! Still, you have to accept some limitations and those around you need to be aware of them if you are to function well.

The inconveniences of Sjögren's generally can be handled by the methods used to treat the symptoms, and preventive vigilance. For the latter purpose, the earliest possible diagnosis is vital.

In particular, there is an antibody [labeled Ro (SSA)] that appears in the blood of some women with Sjögren's syndrome. As it has been noted that there can be an association of this antibody with heart problems in newborn infants,[151],[152] researchers are suggesting that women with SS who become pregnant or are considering having a baby, should ask their doctor about testing for this antibody. The infants may have NLE (neonatal lupus erythematosus) which involves a skin rash that appears at birth but usually heals spontaneously, along with a more serious possibility of heart blockage.

Some patients may have RA factors without having RA or antinuclear antibodies without having lupus.[153] More serious consequences can occur, including the extraglandular manifestations previously discussed, pseudolymphomas (benign), or lymphomas (malignancies), or Waldenstrom's macroglobulinemia (excessive growth of plasma cells.)

I Think, Therefore I Am

How Your Attitude and Your Doctor's Can Help

It's never easy to hear a doctor tell you you have arthritis. In any form. Rheumatoid arthritis. Scleroderma. Or the one with the impossible name, systemic lupus erythematosus. It takes a while to get

---

[151]Frank Arnett *Genes and Predisposition to Rheumatic Disease*

[152]R. Watson et al "A Neonatal Lupus Erythemsatosus: A Clinical Serological and Immunogenetic Study with Review of Literature" *Medicine*; 1984; 63: 362-378

[153]Alexander, M. *Clinical Aspects of Sjögren's Syndrome*323-330

chummy enough with that one to shorten it to lupus. Or just SLE. Each separate kind brings with it frightening images of a future filled with pain and disablement. Or worse imagined horrors. The doctor, being kindly, nevertheless has to say, "We have no cure." You take his prescription, maybe it's just aspirin, and go home feeling very much alone in the world. Chances are you don't know anyone who has arthritis. Oh, Aunt Mabel, maybe, who's all crippled up, but she's old and has always been that way as long as you can remember. You may be thirty five with a full and busy life that has no room in it for chronic illness. Even the term "chronic illness" has such a negative tone to it. It's downright depressing. Or it just makes you mad.

You are hesitant to discuss the doctor's verdict with anyone, even your family, at first. Then eventually you find someone, possibly a friend at work, or in the garden club or church, who also has the same sort of aches and pains, although her brand of arthritis may be different from yours. It helps to have someone to share worries with.

It also helps at this particular time to have an understanding and knowledgeable doctor. He'll be willing to take the time to explain your particular situation to you. He'll tell you honestly and frankly, without unduly frightening you, what your prognosis is and how you can help make it better. If he is prescribing medications, he'll explain to you what they will or will not do for you and what the likely side effects may be. This can be a difficult proposition for him, as there is almost no chemical that we can put into our bodies that will not have multiple effects. He will tell you where the balance lies with the particular medications you need between risk and important help. He will reassure you.

But he will probably wind up saying a lot of it is up to you. You will have to take the medications as he tells you to. You will have to arrange to get the right amount of exercise and rest. But most of all, you will have to adopt a positive attitude. This is far from easy.

Unfortunately, the doctor I have described is not always the one you have to deal with. My files are full of letters from patients who have not had a supportive experience. By far the majority of doctors want to help you adjust, but many are busy. Other patients crowding their waiting room vie for the time you need. Too often the information you get is just the briefest. And the doctor also has to make a judgment call as to how much to tell you. Sometimes he will feel that too much detail will only make your condition more frightening. This is where the idea of partnership comes in. You must let the doctor know that you want to know, that you want to have an active share in the management of your disease. You set the guidelines. He needs to know how much detail you want to assimilate.

Sjögren's syndrome patients have an additional aspect to the problem. Many of my correspondents tell of years of going from one doctor to another in search of an explanation for a myriad of symptoms. Sadly, the tales are all too often of rebuffs. Of being told they are neurotic. Being told, in essence, to go knit something. Anything to keep you busy and out of the long suffering doctor's hair. In defense of the beleaguered doctor, I have to say that he is often up against a wall. As we have seen, SS is a very sneaky disease. It masquerades as rheumatoid arthritis, or lupus, or a number of other things. Or you may actually have one of these other diseases. And in that case the symptoms are likely to be readily identifiable and more immediately serious than the SS symptoms. And the SS symptoms are so diverse the doctors often are unable to correlate them.

The hardest part is achieving a balance in all these things. Having a chronic illness is bad enough in itself, but weeping and wailing about it only makes it worse. Henrietta Aladjem, a lupus patient, writes in The *Journal of the American Medical Association*[154] that her original diagnosis of lupus was particularly frightening, since at that time, in 1953, the disease was considered rare and invariably fatal. "When I didn't die," she says, " the doctors questioned the diagnosis." It has since been learned that lupus is far less rare and far from being universally fatal, but unfortunately, some patients are still being given that fear. SS and each of its companion diseases carry their own fears and worries. Aladjem points out that alleviating these concerns is not an easy task for the doctor. It takes extra time and a real understanding of the patient's life. There are fears that friends and coworkers will find out about this mysterious ailment and think less of its victim for it, or, conversely, that they will not know, and consider the inevitable fatigue just a case of malingering. The patient may fear being shut out of the mainstream, or being unable to keep pace and compete. He finds it difficult to explain problems to his boss or coworkers as much as to the doctor. As he tries he sees their expressions change from attentiveness to obvious annoyance. He may even begin to doubt the reality of his own confusing symptoms. It is especially hard then to be sure the doctor does understand. Patient and doctor both find it equally hard to define where the line is between

---

[154]Henrietta Aladjem"Psychosocial Aspects of Rheumatic Disease - a patient speaks" *Primer on the Rheumatic Diseases* 8th ed. Atlanta GA: Arthritis Foundation; 1983; 205-206

an illness that verges on neurosis, and a neurosis that feeds the illness. Self doubt, guilt, and a physician who places too much emphasis on the mental aspects of the symptoms can be very destructive. My correspondents often tell me they have spent many visits with a psychiatrist, before or after their diagnosis. Some say these sessions make them feel better about themselves but do little to help the disease. Others swear by the value of the counseling they receive. Rose Thomas, a nursery owner in Chesterland, Ohio, kept a diary of her experiences on the road to diagnosis. In 1982 she experienced blurred vision and difficulty swallowing. Visits to an optometrist and an internist brought tests but little relief. She saw an ophthalmologist in 1983 when a Schirmer test revealed no tears, but no diagnosis was made and artificial tears were suggested. Extreme fatigue in 1984 prompted a regimen of estrogen, but the symptoms continued in 1985. Rose saw eight doctors in 1986 but could not clear up her constant sore throat until February of that year when doctors at University Hospital in Cleveland performed a lip biopsy and gave her the diagnosis of Sjögren's syndrome. They told her it was "incurable, untreatable, not known to go into remission, *but* livable." By July, the "throat, the eyes, fatigue, pain seemed to be everywhere," and she could not cope. She was referred to a clinical psychiatrist whose suggestions consisted of relaxation through breathing exercises along with instructions for living one day at a time. Rose finds this very effective and says she highly recommends counseling. She also reports that the support group is extremely valuable and she includes prayer in her regular routine.

All this indicates that, though we all know that SS is certainly not "all in the mind," a patient's mental attitude can and does make a tremendous difference in her ability to manage her Sjögren's and to live a full and rewarding life. Studies by husband and wife team Ronald Glaser and Janice Kiecott-Glaser of Ohio State University indicated that men and women involved in divorces or unhappy marriages had weakened immune systems and lowered ability to fight off infections. But, in a possible explanation of the comfort found in sharing experiences with members of the SS support groups, another study concluded that talking about emotional problems actually strengthened a person's immune responses.[155] This study was reported to the American Psychological Association's 1987 meeting by Southern Methodist University's Jamie Pennebaker

Achieving a healthful mental state is not easy with Sjögren's syndrome, but it can, and must be done. Your doctor, friends, family, and fellow sufferers can all help, but ultimately it is your own outlook and approach to life that will make the difference, and minimize that second problem that comes with the territory. If we can't get rid of the darn syndrome, at least we can learn to live with it.

[155]AP/New York "Immune Systems Linked to Marriage" Houston Post ; 29 August 1987

PART II - How to Outsmart SS

Chapter 9 - You and Your Doctor

From the moment your doctor says "You have Sjögren's syndrome," you have a one on one relationship that must run smoothly to allow you to "live with the disease" as you are often told you must. Actually it may begin well before that, depending on the course of your individual journey to diagnosis. If you are one of those many who have visited a great number of different doctors in different specialties before that magic moment, then this is indeed a shiny new relationship. Of course there are also those examples where one doctor has traveled the road with you all the way, helping you to follow a variety of clues that eventually lead to the SS diagnosis.

In any case it is important to understand how this can be a real partnership in managing your disease and steering your course to health. Far too many of your letters have begun, "In the last five years I have seen six internists, three ophthalmologists, a gastroenterologist and two rheumatologists before one finally said 'Sjögren's syndrome.'" Hopefully that will one day become a thing of the past as more and more doctors are becoming aware of the systemic nature of SS and, whatever their specialty, are on the alert for the signs and symptoms.

Now that you know about SS, how can you best co-operate with your doctor? Or doctors? The first rule is one of disclosure and information. It is your responsibility to keep your doctor informed. As we have commented before, a urologist is not likely to be curious about the state of your eyes unless you give him reason to be. Tell him. Up front. "Doctor, I have Sjögren's syndrome". Then he will know that what appears to be a urinary infection, may, in fact, be a case of interstitial cystitis. In SS more than some other ailments, you are almost certain to be seeing a number of specialists. Usually an internist or a rheumatologist will be your primary care physician, but you will need to have more frequent regular visual and dental checkups than the average person. You may also be seeing a gynecologist, a urologist, a kidney specialist, and/or a dermatologist. The first question you should ask a new doctor is "Do you often treat SS patients?" The first thing you say to your old doctors after your diagnosis is "I have SS."

One problem many of us face is that our doctor is busy and in the rush of the visit, we forget to tell him that one item that has been most on our mind. This is the time for list making. No, you must not succumb to "medical student's disease." Just from reading about them you are likely to think you have every ache and pain mentioned. But wait a while. Set aside this book for a few days so your mind is not cluttered with all the "possibilities" mentioned in it. And then, make your list.

Better yet, why not draw your doctor a picture? Make a simple diagram of the human body (or photocopy the one in Figure 24). Now over a period of time, shortly before your next doctor's visit, just make marks wherever you have a problem. Use the spaces provided to make specific notes. For instance, "Eyes dry - need drops two or three times during night" or "Stiffness in the morning...goes away after I get up and move around." By making these notes as they occur to you, you won't be as likely to forget them when it's time to report to the doctor. Write your list on the palm of your hand if you have to. Use anything that makes it easier for you to be sure your doctor knows all of your problems.

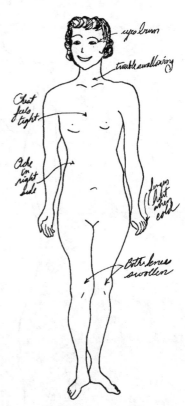

Dr. Carol Beals has suggested a set of questions to ask your doctor about medications he prescribes for you. (I have added a few).

What is the purpose of this drug?

What is it supposed to do?

What are its side effects? Is it a beta blocker?

When should I take it? With or without food?

Figure 23 Figure Showing Complaints

Should I avoid certain foods? Alcohol? Other drugs?

Am I likely to be allergic to it?

Will it make me drowsy?

What should I do if I miss a dose?

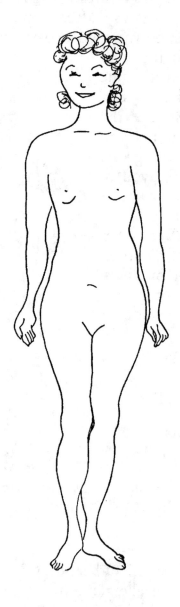

Figure 24 Figure to Note Symptoms for Doctor.

Should I discontinue it when I feel better?

How should I store it? In refrigerator?

Another list that can be helpful is a list showing your current medication schedule. Sure, your doctor should have this information in his file. But you can put it right there on one piece of paper so that he doesn't have to thumb through what may eventually be a pretty large file.

While you're about it, another good idea is to give him a list of your other doctors. Include names, addresses and phone numbers. Communication between your doctors is at times crucial, and if they already have the list in your file it can save a lot of time and trouble.

We have to overcome the urge to answer his "How are you? with "Fine, thanks." Much as we hate to be complainers, this is the time to get it all out. He can't possibly solve your problems if he doesn't know about them.

Chapter 10 - Carrying On

Keeping Track of Medications

All right, you say, maybe I need a list of those medications myself. True. With the complexity of SS and the variety of symptoms that need tending to, your list of medications can sound like a shopping list for your local pharmacist. My list contains eleven separate items. Not all of these are prescriptions. Some are over-the-counter vitamins, calcium, etc. But it's important that your doctors know these too. And if you are using artificial tears or saliva and antacids they belong on your list, too.

To make matters even more complicated, some prescriptions may call for two tablets a day, one every other day or three a week. I have one medication I take one a day for two weeks, then none for the next two weeks. A simple way to keep track of all this, is to use a seven-day pill box. Seven separate compartments can hold a days supply each and be custom tailored for the right day of the week. I fill mine every eight days, keeping the pills for the current day in a smaller box I can carry with me in my purse. You can even get one that is divided into twenty-eight compartments, four for each day of the week. If you have trouble remembering to take your medications or using your eye drops on schedule during the day, there are inexpensive watches and pill boxes available with multiple alarms that can be set to remind you (See Chapter 12, Non-medical techniques). For those medications you take for twenty-five days each month (estrogen), or two weeks on and two weeks off (Didronel); post a calendar someplace handy, like the back of a kitchen cabinet door. Use colored markers to show which days are which and refer to this when you fill your seven-day box. Sounds complicated, but it's a system that works.

Remember also that keeping track has to include remembering to order new supplies. How you do that depends on your source. For some of us, it's just a matter of calling the local druggist and then stopping by to pick it up on the way to the supermarket. Or maybe the druggist is in the supermarket. Others have been introduced to mail order houses by insurance companies trying to contain costs. If your insurance does not cover prescriptions, mail order is an excellent way to save. When you buy by mail, you have to remember to order a week or more before you run out.

Managing Fatigue

Perhaps the most commonly heard complaint about SS is the fatigue that is part and parcel of it. It's important to realize that there can be many causes for fatigue. You could be failing to get enough sleep. Or you could be undernourished. Or maybe your are simply working too hard. There are some medical problems that should be ruled out before ascribing your fatigue to SS. Your doctor will consider hyperthyroidism, anemia, and poor sleep patterns as possibilities. If these have been ruled out and he says, it's just part of the syndrome, there are still some things you can do. Of course the obvious thing is *not* to try to do too much. If you are a perfectionist who is trying to be superwoman, you will be tired. This is the time to think about a credo put forth for Parkinson's disease patients by author Sidney Dorros[156]. He aims for "Acommodation without surrender." By this he means that it can be more productive to recognize your limitations and work to do the best you can within them. This may mean doing jobs in segments. I will clean two rooms of my house today, and two tomorrow, rather than getting all fired up and trying to finish the whole job in one day. A large yard that needs mowing can be done in parts, too. You will find that you can actually accomplish just as much that way because you are working at half speed or less when you are exhausted. And you make mistakes that must be corrected later, costing more time than the rest period would have.

Try to plan your days so that there is time scheduled in for naps, or at least, resting. It's a good idea to make it the same time every day. That way you can rest *before* you get exhausted. Possibly that one special soap opera you just *have* to watch each day could be good for your health!

You don't have to actually go to bed. Just choose a comfortable couch or even a chair and sink into it. A garden lounge chair in a favorite spot can often be the ideal place.

If you don't have a garden, you may want to imagine one. This might be particularly helpful for the mental rest that's just as important as the physical relaxation. Conjure up a quiet nook with periwinkles

---

[156]Sidney Dorros, *Parkinson's: A Patient's View* Seven Locks Press Cabin John MD 1981, p. xviii

blowing in a gentle breeze. Or be creative. You can even have flowers in this garden that wouldn't possibly grow in the climate of your real back yard. Once you've settled on the place and time, just do it. Don't make too big a deal of it. It is supposed to be restful. Get comfortable. A couple of pillows might help. Put one under your knees if your legs are tense. As with all advice in this book, I am assuming you will check with your doctor if you have any conditions which complicate your situation. If you have back pain, for instance, take that into consideration.

Now, try to consciously unwind. There is a soft, drifting kind of a feeling that is the beginning of sleep. That may be all you need. Just float away from the world around you.

Music may help. Choose your favorite tape or disc or turn on the local easy listening radio station. Play classical or sentimental music if that's what you like. It doesn't matter as long as you like it. Maybe some people who grew up with rock and roll can actually be lulled to sleep by it, but probably marching bands are not a good plan. Keep the volume low. There are also tapes available with soothing sounds of waves on the seashore, or birds chirping in the forest. Maybe the crackling noises of a fireplace fire would do it for you. Some people use "white noise" which is a kind of soft static designed to blank out other annoying noises like the ringing in your ears of tinnitus.

Listen to recorded books. The actors who perform them may not appreciate this but a steady voice reading to you can often lull you to sleep. Remember reading your children to sleep at nap time? How many times was it you who first succumbed to your own dulcet tones?

In any case you must clear your mind of chores and worries. Try to derail whatever train of thought you've been wrestling with. If you need them, use the special relaxation techniques described in Chapter 12.

I can hear some of you hooting at the notion of having to go to all that trouble. For some (most?) the real problem is trying not to fall asleep. The advice about establishing a preferred time and place still holds. Just be sure it's really handy. When the fatigue hits you, you need to be able to flop down and abandon the world. This can be difficult if you have young children. The only answer I know then is to coordinate your nap time with theirs. Don't do as I did. I would put the babies down to sleep and then say, "I'll just finish the dishes and then rest." But somehow those I'll-just-finish chores would stretch out so that by the time I was ready to stretch out, the little ones would be waking up and raring to go.

What it all boils down to is you have to make your own adjustments. Do make them, it's worth it and it's absolutely necessary. Never feel guilty about arranging to get that rest. It pays off.

Chapter 11 - Relationships

There are legions of social workers, psychologists, and writers who have made whole careers out of advising people how to get along with other people. There is even a whole genre of books written specifically about how to live with chronic illness. Many of these are excellent and very helpful to Sjögren's syndrome patients. (See Appendix IV: References). But I am going to try to restrict my comments here to suggestions that specifically apply to SS.

Husband and Kids

Probably the single most destructive aspect of SS to relationships is that extreme fatigue most of us deal with. It doesn't show and therefore, it can be hard for our friends to accept. Our kids don't understand why we are not eager to run to the park to play when they come home from school. Our husband expects a bright and perky companion to greet him after work. Even the most understanding of spouses might just flop into his easy chair, saying, "How about a drink?" and expect it to be delivered promptly. We've already discussed ways to handle the fatigue, but you need to concentrate on handling other people's perception of it. Of course, education is your best weapon. Try to convince your spouse and kids to read this book. Join the National Sjögren's Syndrome Association (NSSA) and share the newsletter

(*Sjögren's Digest*) and Patient Education Series articles with them. Get hold of a copy of the NSSA video (*Living Well With Sjögren's Syndrome.*) Or get them to come to a support group meeting with you. If they know that you are one of maybe four million people with this problem, it will be easier to believe. Having them talk to your doctor would be good, *if* you have a doctor who has the time and empathy for that. Perhaps a combination of these ideas would be best of all. Have them come to a support group meeting when a medical speaker is giving an overall view of SS.

Once you have them convinced, it is a matter of letting them know you are doing what you can to accommodate them as well as your illness. This takes some subtlety. There is a fine line between complaining too much and stoically bearing it all in silence. Your loved ones need to know what you are feeling. They need to know if your joints hurt severely or if you have difficulty eating certain foods. On the other hand, if you make their life unpleasant with constant reminders, that will backfire and everyone will be unhappy. This requires a balance that only the individual will know how to find. But you will probably be surprised how understanding they will be, as long as they known as much as possible about your SS.

Bob Treat, whose wife has fibromyalgia, tells her over and over again not to apologize for needing a back rub, or telling him how she feels. "There should be no guilt." He says, "No one has done anything wrong." He no longer tries to achieve perfect harmony or complete order, but tries to help her relax and ease the tensions.[157]

This, as all of those other coping books will tell you, is the place for a positive attitude. Sjögren's syndrome, like any chronic disease, is with you for a lifetime. In spite of all the wonderful research discussed earlier in this book, there is still no magic bullet. But if we can accept our difficulties and even joke about them, others around us will be glad to be around us, and we, too, will find them easier to bear.

Coping for Two

What do you do when your spouse has his/her own chronic illness? You cope. And you could draw closer than ever by your shared or complementary needs. You could have what is known in the scientific world as a symbiotic relationship. You scratch my back and I'll scratch yours.

Everything said in the previous paragraphs applies double here. Now you must not only teach him about your problems, but you must learn all you can about his. Find out what are his strengths and weaknesses and match them to yours. (Isn't that what any good marriage is about?) If necessary, sit down and make lists. Compare needs and abilities and make the most of them.

An example of this comes from my own situation. I call it my "Jack Sprat and his Wife Salad Solution." My husband, Vern, has Parkinson's disease, and one of his problems is that tremors often cause difficulty keeping

[157]Bob Treat "Fibromyalgia...a Spouse's View" *Arthritis Foundation Florida Chapter Newsletter.*Vol XXI. No 2 pp6-7

food on a fork. A tossed salad with a runny dressing can be a disaster. I, on the other hand, with my Sjögreny teeth and dry mouth, have trouble eating lettuce and certain other crunchy veggies like carrots or radishes. So I fix our salads separately, each in its own bowl. I fix his as finger foods with a thick dip instead of dressing. I get the soft stuff. The worst offender for Vern is tomatoes which tend to spill their gooey insides all over his shirt front. So I cut wedges, putting the pulpy parts in my salad and the firm outer section in his. It works great.

He sometimes has difficulty tying shoelaces so I help. I let him do the carpet cleaning because the fumes bother my congested airways. Each couple will find their own ways to adjust and the very act of adjusting can be a plus for both.

Sex

Here is where Sidney Dorros' "accommodation without surrender" is a must. Adjustments of your lifestyle and your expectations can ease problems SS can inflict on a marriage, especially in the area of sexual activity. The problems can be either physical or psychological. In the first category there are three major ways Sjögren's syndrome can influence the sexual aspects of your relationship: pain, dryness and, of course, the ever present fatigue.

Obviously, if your joints hurt, you may be tentative about taking an active part. A sore mouth is a definite downer. In Raynaud's phenomenon, sexual excitement can make the pain worse. It is the constriction of blood vessels and the resulting shortage of blood in the fingers that causes the pain of Raynaud's. During sex the blood rushes to the genital area leaving even less available for the fingers.[158] All of these things can make you hesitate even if you really do want to participate. And your partner may be afraid to hurt you more.

You can ease the situation by planning ahead. If you take pain medications, try to time it so that you will be as comfortable as possible. Try to get some extra rest in the afternoon before a romantic evening. A warm bath helps to relax you and a shared tub or shower is even better. If vaginal dryness is your major problem, reread Chapter 6 for treatment ideas such as lubricating gels.

One psychological aspect was mentioned earlier: the partner's fear of hurting the SS patient. Another is the patient's own lack of self esteem, the feeling that because of the illness she is somehow not as good as she should be, maybe no longer attractive. Taking prednisone does tend to cause you put on weight.

The best answer here is communication. How do you know your spouse thinks less of you? Ask. You may be pleasantly surprised with the answer. And it will help to tell your partner what hurts and what feels good. There are many ways to express sexuality and it's perfectly all right to use them. Even if completing the sex act becomes impossible, you do not have to give up a warm and exciting relationship with your spouse. And by the way, did you know that sexual arousal actually stimulates the production of natural cortisone, with a convenient pain killing effect.

If talking it out doesn't work for you, do try to get professional counseling. I know there are some who fear

[158] Robert H. Phillips *Coping with Lupus* Avery Publishing Group Inc., Wayne NJ 1984 p212

the loss of spontaneity will ruin the pleasure, but there are ways to compensate and they are worthwhile.[159]

On the Job

Relationships with the boss can be another matter. In nine jobs out of ten, the boss' responsibility is to see that as much work per person gets done as possible. His personality and the pressures upon him from above and outside have a lot to do with his attitude towards SS. First of all, our old friend education is an absolute must. All those things you did to clue your family in are extra important here. Your livelihood could depend on his understanding.

Again the chief bugaboo is fatigue. Back in the "good old days" before women's equality, there used to be a law that said an employer had to supply a couch in the ladies room and allow women to rest periodically if needed! That special privilege went by the wayside, and to a certain extent justifiably so. A man with chronic fatigue as in SS needs rest just as much as a woman does. How you can get it depends a lot on your workplace. If you are in a situation where you have a private office and a secretary, you might have a couch in your office (or at least a comfortable chair) where you can catch a fast nap between clients. Dr. Carol Beals, a rheumatologist who has SS, has such a couch. She tells her secretary not to disturb her and sets a kitchen timer for ten minutes so she can lie down when the exhaustion sets in.

---

[159] Sefra Kobrin Pitzele *We Are Not Alone: Learning to Live With Chronic Illness* Workman Publishing, New York 1986pp179189

If there is no handy secluded place where you can actually lie down, you'll have to find other ways. Perhaps, with very understanding co-workers you could just put your head down on your desk. If this is not possible, getting up and walking around (to the coffee urn?) could chase the cobwebs away for the moment.

Much has been said about the use of computers in the workplace (or at home for that matter.) Carpal tunnel syndrome and repetitive motion syndrome (repetitive stress injuries - RSIs) are problems for many otherwise healthy office workers. RSIs made up over half of all work-related injuries in 1990,[160] a fact that helps make employers more understanding. these injuries can be very expensive in terms of medical expenses and lost work hours.

RSIs can become major concerns for SS patients. Painful stressed wrists make typing a nightmare. Staring at the monitor screen all day can be very hard on dry, irritated eyes. Back strain can result from improper posture.

Carpal tunnel syndrome is not necessarily related to SS but can be caused by the swelling of inflamed tissues in the carpal tunnel, an area in the wrist composed of bones and other tissues. The pain occurs when pressure affects the median nerve which runs through the tunnel and sends messages to the brain. Repeated motions like typing, golf, factory chores, or even knitting can produce the stress. The symptoms include pain, tingling and numbness and treatment involves the use of splints to immobilize the wrist and aspirin, NSAIDs, or cortisone. Changing the activity that brought it on

---

[160]*Arthritis Foundation Florida Chapter Newsletter* Vol. Xxi, No.2 p1

helps, and in severe cases, surgery can relieve the pressure on the nerve.

Simple measures can usually alleviate or completely avoid these types of problems. Most important of all is the relationship of your body to the work surface and equipment. Be sure first that your chair gives support and is adjusted to a comfortable height in regard to your desk. Wrist pads placed in front of your computer keyboard can relieve strain on the bones of your wrist and there are stick-on pads available to place at points of contact on your mouse (if you use one.) Then consider lowering and tilting your computer screen so that you can look down on it. Tests done by Dr. Kasuo Tsubota in Tokyo, showed that people looking at a computer screen tend to blink three times less often than when relaxing, allowing the tear film to dry out. But when you look down, your eye openings are smaller and your tear film dries more slowly[161]. Not to mention that having to tilt your head back can lead to a constant stiff neck.

Most SS patients learn early on to make sure of their supply of fluids to drink and drops for their eyes. It's a simple matter to keep your eye drops handy. I use a small glass (a shot glass is perfect) to hold 3 or 4 single unit doses of unpreserved drops on my desk. Your co-workers will soon get used to the sight of you leaning your head back to instill the drops. Of course there are jobs where this might be frowned on. In that case just step out to the rest room. If you need the drops too often for that to be feasible, try finding an activity that let's you turn your back to the area of public view.

---

[161]Kasuo Tsubota, "Researchers: Lower, tilt screen to prevent computer eye strain" Associated Press, *Palm Beach Post* 26 Feb. 1993

Check those file cabinets behind your desk. If you must have the drops while a client is watching, simply explain, "I have dry eyes. This helps." That's better than allowing the irritation to continue, with possible harm to your eye. Most people will be understanding. Glasses with a slight tint can help shield against glare from screen or overhead lights. Ultra violet film protection is useful even in artificial light.

For the dry mouth, there's always a container of water or a package of sugar-free candies. If you put the candies in an attractive dish on your desk, your clients will think you are being very considerate of them. If you drink colas, try to use the sugar-free kind, to protect your teeth.

Even without SS, many people keep moisturizing lotion in their desk drawer for their dry hands. And I know one man who keeps an electric foot vibrator under his desk, to provide a hidden change from that all day sitting position and get that blood circulating. Trouble is, it sounds like a model train going through the office, and that can be disconcerting!

I realize there are many other situations in which the solutions may not be so easy. One patient wrote that he was a salesman and had great difficulty doing his job because his throat was dry and talking was hard for him. Another, a stockbroker, has had to give up her work.

The whole job question brings up an important principle. If you have any problems that interfere with your normal functioning, you do not *necessarily* have to give up. Discuss your Sjögren's syndrome matter-of-factly with associates, but don't harp on it. Assess the demands of your job and try to analyze your continuing ability to perform them. If you truly feel it has become impractical to continue in your present job, think of other options. Perhaps you can use your experience in ways that are less demanding or distressing. A fabric salesperson may find the sizing dust too irritating for her eyes, but could easily work in a china department where there would be less air pollutants.

Possibly you and your employer can work out a flexible time arrangement if your duties allow. If you could work part time, or arrange to take those rest breaks on a regular basis, it might be a very efficient set up, as beneficial to the company as to you. Do you know anyone else with similar skills who would like to work part time? Job sharing has worked very well in some cases.

Sidney Dorros says "If I knew then what I know now, I might have had a happier and longer work experience."[162] His message is simply not to give up , but to look for those aids and alternatives that can help keep you in the work force as long as possible.

---

[162] Sid and Donna Dorros *Patient Perspectives on Parkinson's* National Parkinson Foundation Miami 1992 p39

Chapter 12 - Non-medical Techniques

In treating any chronic illness everybody concerned wants to use as little medical intervention as possible. We should certainly take what ever medications the scientists and physicians have found that will help correct our medical problems. And in those cases (rare in SS) where surgery can make the difference, that too, is a good thing. But techniques that ease our pain or moisten our dry parts without pills or knives, are most welcome. And fortunately, there are options available for SS patients.

Physical Therapy

Some patients whose joint pains are not being satisfactorily managed by anti-inflammatory drugs or low level pain medications may benefit from physical therapy. If you've ever walked past the PT department of your local hospital, you've seen an amazing array of machines looking like a workout gym gone slightly askew. There are chairs with attachments to give passive motion exercise to an injured leg. There are parallel bars for walking and stretching exercises. There are hot tubs and padded exercise mats and weight lifting machines. Most of these are involved in rehabilitation. Stroke patients, accident victims, and many others benefit from them.

But the techniques that apply especially to SS patients include heat, cold, ultrasound, and electrostimulation. Joint pain is one of the major effects of SS. Remember the triad of symptoms? Dry eyes, dry mouth, and arthritis. If you have any two of the three types of symptoms, you were considered to have Sjögren's syndrome. Arthritis, as we have learned, is joint pain. And the techniques listed above can often help those aching joints.

Pain has long been poorly understood and difficult to measure In 1965 the *gate control* theory was proposed to say that there is a mechanism in the spinal cord that can increase or decrease the flow of pain messages from the source of the pain to the brain.[163] If there is no interference, the full force of the pain reaches the brain and is felt. If there are other nerve signals equal to or greater than the pain, there is less pain felt. That's why counter irritation can help. In other words, if you feel more of another sensation, you feel less of the original pain. If someone steps on your toe, you will not feel the ache in your hand so severely.

What the therapist tries to do is add other, *non*-painful sensations to drown out the pain. Heat and cold both serve to stimulate nerves in the skin and lessen pain by sending competing messages to the brain. Both lead to muscle relaxation and are effective in relieving pain. The application of cold will reduce muscle spasm but can take longer than you would like. Heat can be applied directly to the skin with hot packs, paraffin baths, or in a whirlpool, or as radiant heat from infrared lamps.

---

[163] R. Melzack and P D Wall "Pain mechanisms: A new theory" Science 150:971, 1985

A soak in a heated whirlpool tub can be done at home, if you are fortunate enough to have one. It can relax those tense muscles and help the pain immensely. The hot tub is an excellent way to get rid of that famous morning stiffness that often goes with arthritis. Again care is essential to avoid burns. Water temperatures should not exceed 102°F (38.9°C) to 105°F (40.5°C).[164] Your hot tub should have a thermometer that can be checked before entering the bath. Doing mild exercises, such as bicycle kicks, in the water makes it even more effective. A hot bath in your ordinary tub will work well, too.

Heat from infrared lamps, like the one you often find in better hotel bathrooms, can be very soothing. As can electric heating pads. A pad that can be wrapped around the hurting area (like a knee) can be strapped on with velcro. Both of these items are readily available at your local drugstore. Caution should be used where there is the possibility of falling asleep with the heating pad on. A control that must be pressed to make the pad heat will provide a safety factor.

For pain that won't go away, your doctor may recommend a course of ultrasound and electrostimulation in addition to applied heat, by professional therapists, usually as an outpatient at a hospital.

Paraffin baths are most often used to soothe the aching joints of hands or feet. A tank of the wax is heated to a comfortable temperature and the hands are dipped into it. The emphasis here is on "comfortable" temperature, as too-hot wax can cause serious burns. The usual level of 118°F (47.0°C) to 130°F (54.4°C)

---

[164]Mark T. Walsh "Hydrotherapy: The Use of Water as a Therapeutic Agent" Thermal Agents in Rehabilitation Ed. Michlovitz F. A. Davis Company Philadelphia 1990, p129

sounds hot but when the paraffin is mixed with mineral oil, it is a tolerable range. This procedure should only be done in the PT department or with proper training and supervision. A special table top paraffin unit is available for home use, but trying it at home with do-it-yourself methods could be dangerous, as sensitivity to heat varies from person to person and the patient is not always the best judge.

Ultrasound gets the heat deeper into the tissues, getting more at the source of the pain. Sound is created when molecules are set in motion, one bumping against the next, causing a vibrational energy. The movement of these molecules causes the heating effect. Ultrasound is sound with a frequency too high for humans to hear. It has been used for medical treatment since the late 1930s. This should also be used in the PT department and under your doctor's instructions. Proper analysis of the patient's condition is essential, as use of ultrasound on an acutely inflamed joint could make it worse

In the course of the treatment an instrument with a flat metal knob called a transducer is used. The therapist will first apply a gel to the area to be treated. This helps transfer the energy to the patient by eliminating as much air as possible from between the transducer and the patient's skin. Sometimes the transducer will be held in one place, or it may be moved around making a pleasant sensation similar to a massage. The sound energy penetrates more deeply into the body than simple radiated heat can, making it particularly useful for alleviating pain in the spine. Since the effect of ultrasound is relaxation of muscles, it is often used in combination with stretching and strengthening exercises.

Electrostimulation is pretty much what it sounds like. In this case electrical currents are the source of the energy that heats the affected tissues. There are a variety of methods of using electrical energy. In some cases electrodes are placed on the area (lower back, for instance) with some material in between that allows the energy to be safely transferred.

Exercise

Exercise is another very popular subject. Many books, videos and magazine articles constantly tell us we should exercise. They usually also want to tell us how. So, once again there's no need for me to repeat what you can easily find elsewhere. By now we all know how it can help control our weight and give us "great buns."

But it is worth emphasizing how helpful exercise can be in controlling that joint pain. The most common prescription is to walk briskly a half an hour, three times a week. This is probably the easiest advice you'll ever want to follow. It takes no special equipment (except a good pair of walking shoes) and can be done almost anywhere. Most primary Sjögren's syndrome patients are not disabled enough to prevent walking unless there is some other problem involved. For those of you who are more disabled, please forgive me, but also notice the qualifier "primary." If there is rheumatoid arthritis or myositis (muscle weakness) involved, that's a different matter.

Morning stiffness and painful knees or hips can definitely make walking uncomfortable. The rule of thumb that has been proposed is that if it hurts while you are doing it, that's not too bad, but if it still hurts two hours later, you are doing harm and should adjust your activity. Most important, you must use good judgment. "No pain, no gain" is definitely not a good credo for arthritis sufferers. You should not continue any exercise that hurts consistently. If a new form of exercise hurts when you first start, that is most likely just muscle strain, and if the exercise is not overdone, the pain will go away quickly with gradual increase in the use of those muscles.

One way to beat the stress on joints is to do your exercises in water. A slightly heated or sun warmed pool is great because the water not only warms your muscles and joints, its buoyancy offsets some of your body weight. It is much easier to do aerobics that raise the heart rate to the desired point. While some people advocate swimming, it has been suggested that exercising standing up is more effective for the heart since it must pump the blood more than in the horizontal position of swimming.[165]

One important consideration, no matter what form of exercise you decide on, is that it must be enjoyable. Walking with a friend is better than walking alone, unless you have six kids and that's your one time of day to be by yourself. For several years, I had a friend and neighbor to walk with. At that time we each had an aging parent living with us, and our morning walks were excellent therapy. That was our chance to let off steam and compare notes about the problems of sharing our lives with an elderly relative.

Water exercise classes can be very enjoyable. The group I currently exercise with sits and relaxes around the neighborhood pool a while afterwards, providing a good social contact between neighbors. Once a month we go to lunch after the workout. The danger there is

---

[165]Lynette Jamison "The Wave of the Future: Aquatic Exercise" *Newsweek* April, 1993

the temptation to put back on all the calories we burned in the class session.

Of course there are many ways to get the needed exercise. If you have always played golf, or tennis, find a friend who has also slowed down a little so that you play at more or less the same level. In this case it really isn't whether you win or lose but just that you play at all. If you have a mind that likes a set routine, a video tape is ideal. Set a certain schedule (first thing in the morning, Monday, Wednesday, and Friday, for instance). Stick to it.

And that applies to whatever you choose to do. It only works if you keep at it and make it part of your life. You will find your routine becomes so ingrained, you will definitely miss it when something interferes with your schedule.

And if you get discouraged, remember the story of Dvera Berson, author of the book, *Pain-free Arthritis*.[166] Berson states that at sixty-five, she was in constant, disabling pain when she decided to try exercising in a motel swimming pool. It helped so much she developed a special exercise plan. Now 80, she averages 100 lengths of the pool a day, swimming a special stroke she has developed that exercises all the parts of her body that are affected by arthritis. She says she is pain free and she lectures regularly about her program.

Nutrition

Good nutrition goes hand in hand with exercise for feeling good. Again there are many reference books that cover the general subject. We have all been brought

---

[166]Dvera Berson *Pain-Free Arthritis* S & J Books, Brooklyn, NY 1978

up on the basic food groups and the need for three balanced meals per day. That should be obvious, but for many of us it's not that easy. We are constantly bombarded with new theories and new miracle diets, although the latter are usually aimed more at making us thin than at making us healthy. But even the United States government can't seem to make up it's mind about what is good for us and what is not.

There are some specifics that apply to SS and they are generally just common sense. If your mouth is dry, it is logical to stick to moist foods. But that doesn't mean you can just eat gelatin and applesauce because they slide down easily. You still have to consider that balanced diet. But within that limit there is a lot of leeway. You can choose chicken instead of beef or pork because it is usually tenderer when fully cooked, as all meats should be. Avoid food that is gritty or leaves little bits and pieces in your mouth (cornbread, nuts, popcorn.) Actually this is a subjective area, one where you have to decide about the risk/benefit ratio of individual foods. Lettuce may give you fits sticking to your teeth, but you may feel you just have to have a good tossed salad from time to time.

Smaller amounts of food can help stave off that uncomfortable feeling of being stuffed. Dr. Carol Beals recommends eating five small meals (snack-sized) a day rather than three larger ones.

If you have difficulty swallowing, you may no longer have to settle for baby food. The National Cancer Institute publishes a booklet of eating hints and recipes especially designed for people who have a hard time chewing and swallowing. Although produced for cancer patients, the hints apply equally to us and the booklet is free.[167] Maxine Dereiko, a registered dietitian, and Elaine Teutsch, a registered nurse, have collaborated on a collection of recipes especially designed for you. Derieko specializes in solving nutritional problems and Teutsch has SS herself. Their book, *Recipes for Easy Chewing and Safe Swallowing* contains tips and recipes for foods that are easy to swallow.[168] Derieko also co-authored, with Patricia Stout, *Swallowing Safely, Swallowing Nutritiously, a Manual of the Swallowing Impaired.*

But there is a scientific aspect to all this. Dr. Gabriel Fernandes has been studying nutrition and the immune system at the University of Texas at San Antonio. He looks at the immune cells as entities that need nourishment. We have already seen how active they can be so it is not surprising that they need fuel to maintain all that activity. Fernandes' studies have been aimed at determining the effect of various nutritional elements on the functions of the immune system. It is well known that some of these functions deteriorate with severe malnutrition and also with normal aging, bringing greater susceptibility to infections, cancer, and autoimmune diseases. He suggests that any nutritional factors that might delay or reverse this decline, might also delay or modify the development of those diseases.

Studies have indicated that diets rich in fish oil decreased breast cancer tumors in rats, and possibly also in humans. Unfortunately for us, there is not yet any convincing proof that this is true of autoimmune disease. Some RA patients in a study did get some relief

---

[167]*Eating Hints: Recipes and Tips for Better Nutrition During Cancer Treatment* NIH Publication #87-2079 National Cancer Institute, Bethesda MD 20892 1987

[168]Maxine Derieko and Elaine Teutsch *Recipes for Easy Chewing and Safe Swallowing* Derieko-Teutsch & Associates, PO Box 8366, Portland Orgeon.

from joint pain from w-3 fatty acid (fish oil), but this was neither consistent nor dramatic. However, Dr. Fernandes says the quality of the fish oil has not been properly regulated in the past. He has had success in treating animals with improved fish oil which appears to have a non-steroidal anti-inflammatory effect. He is using the fish oil for studies to determine if other similar oils may be practical as cooking oils to provide benefits on a molecular level. A Canadian company is already producing bread made with flax seed oil which has not been heated in the preparation process. Overheating, which frequently occurs in standard cooking oil manufacture, seems to cause the loss of some beneficial components.

Vitamins are considered to protect tissues and cells against oxidation damage, but the exact explanation for this is still being studied. Generally speaking, we are advised to keep our weight down (logical when you think of stress on joints) and eat that wonderful but elusive balanced diet.

Relaxation

Another kind of stress that influences our ability to cope is the kind of tension that may come with emotional problems or may just be the result of trying to get through the "thousand and one activities of our daily round." That wired feeling can make your muscle pain worse and create havoc with already malfunctioning digestive systems. Fortunately, there are experts out there who have thoroughly addressed the subject of dealing with tension. But some general information may be appropriate here.

The stress that we are dealing with occurs when something, good or bad, alerts your body that some action is needed. The starting gun is fired and the racer runs. A glance at the calendar tells us we have only two days to finish an important project. A daughter announces her engagement signaling a major effort to plan her wedding. Our doctor sends us to the hospital for MRI tests to try to identify that pain that won't go away. These things trigger chemical changes that are needed to initiate the required action. As with pain, we cannot do entirely without stress.

But stress that does not lead to action, or continues after the need for action is passed is what harms us. Fortunately, those experts I mentioned have figured out some specific ways to deal with excess stress. Two techniques are described by Kate Lorig and James Fries.

The Jacobson Progressive Relaxation method (mentioned briefly in Chapter 6) was devised by Edmund Jacobson, who reasoned that in order to relax a muscle, you must know what it feels like to be tense. He taught his students to contract their muscles one at a time, consciously feeling the tension in each. After holding the tension for two to five seconds, they were told to release it all at once and feel the relaxation that followed. he set up a series of exercises working with one hand and then the other, and progressing from hand to arm to shoulders, etc. until the whole body is involved. From this you can learn to recognize the tension and just let it go. [169]

A second technique known as the relaxation response was worked out by Dr. Herbert Benson. For this, you choose a quiet situation to tune out the world around you, choose a word or a vision that seems peaceful to you and linger on it, emptying your mind of all

---

[169]Kate Lorig and James Fries *The Arthritis Helpbook* pp107-112

distractions. Do this in a comfortable position for at least 20 minutes.

These and other suggestions are explored in the Arthritis Helpbook and if thoughtfully carried out, can bring a lot of relief from tension. Of course, there are many regimens such as meditation, yoga and tai-chi that have been practiced in the far east for centuries. It's not hard to find classes if you prefer your relaxation to be a group activity. You can relax and make new friends at the same time.

Devices

There are many ingenious inventions that can be lifesavers for the SS patient. Some relieve pain, some help in preventive maintenance and some may actually supply us with the vital moisture we need to function. There are many products for the mouth, some for the eyes and a few that address our other problems. Happily, these are approaches that do not require more medications.

Most of us are familiar with the various teeth cleaning devices such as the WaterPik which sends a strong jet of water between our teeth to serve a similar function to flossing. WaterPik is available in a scaled down version for travel. A small portable water jet called the Aqua Floss 2000, from Tocad America, Inc., is handy for use after away-from-home meals. At about six inches by two inches, the unit is a little bulky but still compact enough to carry in a good sized purse.

There are several electric tooth brushes, including the Interplak rechargeable brush whose clumps of bristles rotate separately. Others are the Braun Oral-B Plaque Remover, Rota-dent, and Plaque Control 2000.

I found several portable versions in Tokyo including one not much larger than a standard toothbrush that operates on one AA battery.

A Philadelphia periodontist, Dr. Henry S. Brenman invented a machine to electrically stimulate the saliva glands. Called the Salitron, it is produced by Biosonics and consists of a unit that operates on a 9 volt battery. There is a probe which, when pressed against the roof of the mouth, causes a tingling sensation and sends this message to the brain which is relayed to the salivary glands. The usual prescription is to use the machine 3 times a day. At $1700 it is not cheap but the cost may be covered for Medicare recipients. As with many treatments for SS, the results vary considerably with the individual. Some get little benefit, but others say their dryness is no longer a problem even years after stopping the use of the Salitron.

A very ingenious solution to the lack of saliva has been designed by Drs. Hans 's-Gravenmade, Arjan Vissink, and M. C. Huisman of Groningen, The Netherlands. They have designed dentures with a reservoir to hold a saliva substitute solution to be dispensed into the mouth as needed. The reservoir can be built into either upper or lower dentures and requires that there be enough space in the mouth that the patient can tolerate the extra thickness. This is an apparently expensive option, but the authors suggest that using an existing denture can save on the cost.

We have already seen a similar item for dry eyes, the reservoir glasses illustrated in Chapter 6. However, Dr. James Bertera of Scheppens Eye Institute at Harvard University has taken that concept into the computer age. Using the principle of the ink jet printer, he has designed glasses with reservoirs that keep the tear supply coming at an even pace. The glasses frame has a built in reservoir, a pump, and a timer. It does not touch the eye but would provide a commercially available tear solution at a controlled rate. Again cost (estimated to be a bit less than $1000) may be a problem, but the designers are working on that, as well as on reducing the size to make it look acceptable cosmetically.

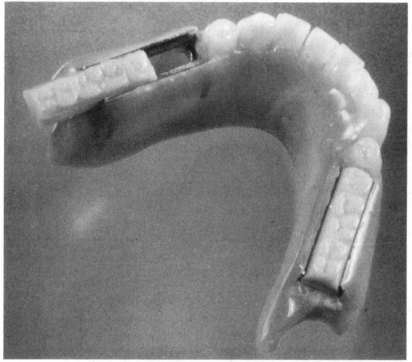

Figure 25 Reservoir Dentures

For those of us looking for less esoteric (and less expensive) solutions, a company called Eagle Vision can supply clear plastic (Moist Eye) moisture panels that your optician can adapt to your glasses and your face. These form protective pockets to keep the natural moisture of the air captured in the space around your eye.

Sun Goggles by Eye Communications or ordinary swimmers goggles can do much the same thing.

A special tip is available for the WaterPik that provides irrigation for the nasal passages. It 's not recommended to use the regular dental tips for the nose as the spray may be too strong and cause injury.

Of course there are any number of vaporizers of the type used for babies that will add moisture to the dry air of our homes to make life more tolerable. Some available brands of these are: Aprilaire Humidifier, Spacegard Air Cleaner, Cool Mist Vaporizer. However, some of us with joint pain may actually prefer the dryness of air-conditioning to ease the pain and increase our energy level.

There are many types of pill boxes designed to make remembering and taking medications easier. Watches are available that have multiple alarms to remind you it's pill time. Walgreen's drugs carries an electronic pill box with a timer/clock. An ingenious gadget, Zelco's Aqua Pill Timer, goes a step further. It is a pill container, an electronic alarm and has a compartment for enough water to take the pills by. It even has a little pop up straw to make drinking easier.

One more gadget that's a freebie deserves mention here. If you or someone you know has a stay in a hospital ask for the little plastic stand the nurse uses to hold you personal thermometer. These little devices make an ideal repository for your single dose eye drops. Just stand the little plastic tube up on end in the indentation meant for the thermometer. (Thanks to Bob Shorr of Miami for that one!)

Chapter 13 - On the Go with SS

Preplanning

There's a lot of information available about making travel easy so we won't need to repeat the basics here. But there are a few things that are especially relevant to Sjögren's syndrome patients. Traveling is tiring for anyone, but if you suffer from chronic fatigue it becomes a real problem. When we are at home, sitting around the dining room table with a dozen tour books and maps spread out we are apt to try to plan to see all of Spain, France, Belgium, and The Netherlands in 17 days. Maybe this can be done if you ride a tour bus that stops no longer than 20 minutes in any one spot, but I'll guarantee you won't enjoy it. The key is to be realistic. We all have parameters. A range of activities we can comfortably accomplish. And sometimes we need to reach out to stretch them, to do more than just what is easy. But our grand tour is not the time for heroics. To see and enjoy the Cathedral of Notre Dame, you don't really *have* to climb all 350 stairs up to get chummy with the gargoyles. A, You don't *really* have to get eyeball to eyeball with them, and B, there's an elevator. Take it.

But what if there isn't an elevator? That's where planning ahead comes in. If you use a travel agent, she/he can help you pick and choose among all the glories of Europe to find the ones that are user friendly. If not, that's what all those guide books are for. Check into the facilities at your chosen attractions. I once traveled all over Europe with a friend who had a phobia about elevators (which was a little odd since at the time she worked on the 51st floor of the Chrysler Building.) My weak knees and I hated climbing stairs. We had a kind of a deal. She walked up; I rode. While she climbed the steps of the leaning Tower of Pisa, I stayed on the ground and watched. I rode the elevator to the top of the Eiffel Tower. In some instances we simply bypassed such things as sky high cable car rides which she could not tolerate. We did fine with these compromises, but might have been better off if we had checked into these things before we left home and had been able to make decisions about them in advance.

If there are must see places on your itinerary that will require a lot of energy, build in opportunities to rest. A cable car takes passengers most of the way up to the base of Corquovado, the statue of Christ on the mountain outside of Rio de Janeiro. From the cable car station to the viewing platform at the base of the huge statue there are 190 steps. About two thirds of the way up there is a landing with benches. Use them and whatever places you can find to take a break and catch your breath.

An important part of your trip plan should be hours, afternoons, or even whole days if needed, set aside to rest. If your traveling companion is likely to have more stamina than you, work that into your advance planning, too. Identify things that each of you is particularly interested in. While you are resting, he can take off alone to see the ones you are not as concerned about. It's important that you have this understanding ahead of time to avoid arguments on the road.

Packing

Almost as important as allowing time to rest, is the planning that helps save energy. Of course the number one thing about packing is don't. That is, don't pack anything more than you absolutely need to have along. Think about the purpose of your trip and who you will see. If you are attending a professional conference you will see colleagues and will need at least one dress-for-success outfit. If you expect to visit friends or relatives along the way, you may need party clothes. But if you are strictly a tourist, the odds are good you will not be seeing anyone you know. That of course, doesn't give license to be an "ugly American," dressing like a slob. However, I have discovered a neat trick. If you have clothes you are just about ready to retire, take some of those with you, wear them a few times hiking among the ruins of Athens, and then toss them. This lightens your luggage, saves laundry and gives more room for those souvenirs you are bound to buy. I started off on one business/pleasure trip where the meeting I attended was at the beginning of the trip and the pure sightseeing came later. I bought new, inexpensive white shoes and bag for my dress outfit. They looked great for the meeting, but soiled quickly with weeks of traveling afterwards. When I no longer needed them for dress, I simply left them for the maid at one of our hotels.

For hard core sightseeing, a normal shoulder bag purse is a lure for sticky fingers and is also unnecessarily heavy to carry. I found the combination of a fanny bag and a back pack useful. But be sure to wear the bag in front of your waist, not behind where it would simply be an invitation to thieves.

Speaking of thieves, why not leave your family heirlooms and valuable jewelry at home. Before one trip I bought a watch at a discount store for $5.00. It kept perfect time for the length of my trip and I didn't have to worry about it. The same holds for any jewelry you really care about. If you must take valuables, be sure to leave them in the hotel safe, along with your passport and emergency cash. Just don't forget, as I did once, that you have left 2 packets in the safe deposit box. The one I left behind held all the gemstones I had purchased in Rio. Fortunately the hotel personnel were honest and forwarded them to me at the next stop.

When planning your wardrobe for the trip, buy the lightest weight clothing possible. Even for wintertime. You can layer sweaters and jackets over dresses or shirts to get the warmth you need. Weight should be a consideration also for luggage. Nylon beats genuine leather any day in my book. I even carry a nylon wallet to minimize weight. It all adds up. The more weight you carry, the more energy you burn.

Medications

But do remember your personal apothecary. If you use, as many Sjögren's Syndrome patients do, a generous array of tablets and capsules, be sure to figure the exact amount you will need for the trip. And then buy twice that many. Put them in two different containers. Always keep one set in the small tote bag you carry with you everywhere. That's the one you do not trust to the airlines, but carry on board the plane with you. With them you should keep a letter from your doctor outlining your drug regimen. Keep that in your tote, too. You may need it if some customs officer questions the amount of little white pills you are bringing into their country.

But don't forget the non-prescription drugs you use. Your eyedrops. Your artificial saliva preparations. Your vitamins, sugar-free candies, laxatives, or anti-gas tablets. You may have trouble finding these in foreign countries. Even in the United States, it could be a time waster to have to shop for these things along the way. That shouldn't have to be part of your itinerary.

I find that seven day pill box that's so handy at home to be even more so when traveling. You tend to lose track of the days and it is harder than ever to keep track of what you are taking on the road. Having each day's complement set aside in advance can be a life saver. Each morning, I take that day's supply out of the main box and put them into a smaller container to put in my fanny (belly) bag. Then I know that at lunch time, those pills are there for me.

Chapter 14 - Other problems, related or not?

Your letters were full of descriptions of the symptoms of Sjögren's syndrome that bothered each of you. And believe me, there was an astonishing variety. Most were well known as part and parcel of the SS package. These, plus some that aren't as easily identified as SS have been discussed in this new version of the book. I hope I haven't missed any. But there were quite a few things mentioned that just cannot be established to be a routine part of the disease. Hopefully, future studies will examine these problems with an eye to settling the question of are they or are they not?

But we can certainly discuss them here. It will be more like a list, because all that really can be done is to tell you someone out there with Sjögren's syndrome is bothered by these problems. They may be symptoms looking for a syndrome, or they may be complete diseases just hitching a ride. But here goes. You wrote that, in addition to all the traditional discomforts of Sjögren's syndrome, some of you suffered from:

AIDS	Fibromyalgia	Pancreatitis
Asthma	Heart problems	Shingles
Back spasms	High cholesterol	Shortness of breath
Chest pain	Hypochondria	Spaced out feelings
Choking	Itching	Stomach ache
Depression	Knot under the ear	Mini-strokes (TIAs)

(Please check the index/glossary for further references to specific items on this list)

The relationship between AIDS and SS (some AIDS patients may have SS-like symptoms) has already been discussed. Some items on the list, such as depression or pancreatitis may well be connected to SS, but cannot arbitrarily be considered caused by the disease. There is a great temptation to attribute every symptom we have to SS, but there is a danger in that. It is too easy to shrug off a stomach ache, saying that's just part of it. The risk there is that you may not make the effort to track down the real cause which could, quite easily, be treatable. Or too serious to ignore.

Meanwhile, the effort to distinguish between SS symptoms and those problems that just happen to bug a person who also has SS goes on. A massive, ongoing survey is being conducted on an international basis to help learn more about the variety of SS symptoms. At the 4th International SS Symposium in Tokyo in 1993, I presented the results of a preliminary study based on the reports of 225 American patients. The answers to over 150 questions showed that the patients on average were younger than is often thought, that their main problems, after the dry eyes and mouth, were fatigue, muscle pain and joint pain. These were followed by digestive, pulmonary, and neurologic symptoms. The surprises were such symptoms as nasal congestion and dryness, gas, and backache. Many of you described having memory lapses, depression and restlessness.

Interestingly, our survey results compared very closely to the results of the *Focus op Sjögren* study done in the Netherlands. It's exciting to think about a possible comparison between these studies and those in other countries to make a truly international picture of the effects of Sjögren's syndrome.

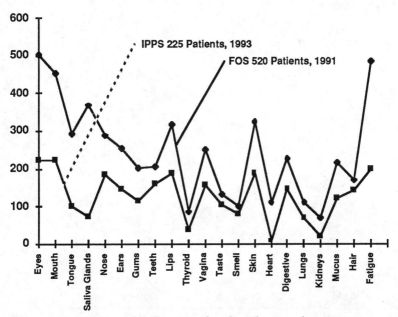

Figure 26 US and The Netherlands Studies Compared
(IPPS = US based survey,
FOS = The Netherlands survey)

Appendix I - Support Resources

Bernice Kapalin, who has been forced by corneal ulcers to leave her job, feels "like a freak because so many people, including some nurses she knows, never heard of SS." Helen Ruhl, who writes that she is "learning to live with her SS," laments that she knows no one else who has it. "I am," she says, "a rare bird."

As we have seen, that may not be so, according to the doctors investigating SS. But loneliness among an invisible crowd is one of the commonplaces of SS. There are hundreds of stories out there of women with sad tales of going from doctor to unsympathetic doctor and feeling more and more lonely and depressed all the time. Please forgive me, I know there are men involved, too, but since SS appears to be partial to women, and there is this unfortunate stereotype of the unfulfilled housewife who turns to hypochondria for solace, most of the stories I've heard come from women. They have gone for months or years being told "You are an emotional woman," "Go home, put your contacts in, and forget about it," or "It's all part of menopause." Even after you get a diagnosis of SS, it seems no one's ever heard of it and you feel very much alone. Often husbands and children have grown tired of hearing about your problems and it seems, as Kapalin put it, hardly worth going grocery shopping and cooking when "I can't taste anything anyway."

Support Organizations

If you fit into that lonely category, take heart. There are others who understand how you feel. And many have banded together to form support groups. These may be independent groups or chapters affiliated with a larger organization such as the National Sjögren's Syndrome Association.

National Sjögren's Syndrome Association

Formed in February of 1990 by a few Sjögren's syndrome patients, the NSSA is dedicated to providing information for all who are interested in Sjögren's syndrome. This is accomplished through the Sjögren's Digest, a quarterly newsletter and the Patient Education Series, a compendium (also mailed quarterly) of articles by authorities on the various aspects of Sjögren's syndrome.

Symposia are held regularly in different parts of the country. Representatives of NSSA attend the major medical association conferences to spread the word on SS to health professionals and keep track of the latest research. The founding officers were Barbara Henry, Betsy Latiff, Harriett P. Miller, Anitaraye Shehi, Catherine K. Sheehan, and Bonnie T. Litton. A distinguished panel of international authorities form the Association's Medical Advisory Board. There are representatives or affiliates in many countries, including Japan, Brazil, Argentina, France, Denmark, Canada, and Australia. There are chapters or resource persons in many parts of the United States and the rate of growth is such that by the time this goes to press there will surely be many more chapters in many cities across the country and around the world. If there still is not one near you, you can find help in forming one by contacting NSSA. Meetings for most chapters are held regularly, with leading physicians and researchers serving as speakers. Topics covered range from specifics about the care and feeding of dry eyes to discussions of the problems of coping with chronic disease. Speakers' specialties include dentistry, immunology, gynecology, dermatology, and many more areas that can be affected by SS.

The Sjogren's Syndrome Foundation Inc.

As early as 1983 in a time when Sjögren's Syndrome was almost completely unknown to the general public, the Sjogren's Syndrome Foundation was formed at the Long Island Jewish Community Center, under the auspices of the Arthritis Foundation by a group of patients led by Elaine Harris. From that small beginning the current organization grew to have many chapters in the US and in many other parts of the world. The SSF publishes a monthly newsletter, *The Moisture Seekers* and *The Sjogren's Syndrome Handbook,* a compilation of chapters on SS by doctors who are specialists in the various fields affected by the disease. As with other support organizations, education and the promotion of research are major goals of the SSF. As Executive Director, Harris attends many medical conventions and presents symposia for SS patients.

The Arthritis Foundation

An organization which deals with the concerns of all 109 varieties of arthritis (or more properly, connective tissue diseases) is the Arthritis Foundation. Headquartered in Atlanta, Georgia, it supports scientific research, promotes public information and education, and gives direct aid to people in the community who suffer from rheumatic diseases. The Arthritis Foundation cooperates with the American Rheumatism Society, a professional organization of rheumatologists, and the Arthritis Health Professions Association, whose members consist of nurses, physical and occupational therapists, medical social workers and others. Local chapters in many cities conduct seminars and sponsor support groups. A program of self help courses to aid in coping have been conducted in many cities. The foundation distributes, free, a series of pamphlets concerning many aspects of arthritis (including one on Sjögren's syndrome) and uses in its self-help courses two books, *Arthritis; a Comprehensive Guide* by Dr. James F. Fries, MD., [170] Director of the Stamford Arthritis Clinic, and *The Arthritis Helpbook* by Kate Lorig, RN., Dr. P.H. [171] and Dr. Fries. Although these do not include information specific to Sjögren's syndrome, the two books contain much information that does apply to our problems. In addition, the foundation maintains a list of recommended books on various aspects of arthritis, with books rated by a star system, but the list has not been updated since 1987.

Other publications of the AF include their national magazine, *Arthritis Today,* and newsletters published by the local chapters. The magazine contains articles by doctors and journalists relating to the business of living with arthritis and even some fiction. There are regular

---

[170]Fries *Arthritis*
[171]Lorig *Helpbook*

features bringing updates on the state of the world in terms of arthritis. The AF provides research fellowships and helps support research institutions and community centers throughout the country. The local newsletters bring news of seminars and other activities of your local chapter.

Another service provided by the Arthritis Foundation can be particularly helpful for secondary SS patients with debilitating rheumatic disease. The organization's local branches maintain equipment loan closets. They will lend such equipment as wheelchairs at no charge to those who need them. For patients in search of a doctor, they maintain a list of area rheumatologists. They cannot recommend a specific doctor, but can help you learn which doctors specialize in arthritis type diseases and which maintain offices convenient to you.

NORD

Another organization that can be helpful to Sjögren's syndrome interests is NORD, the National Organization for Rare Disorders. In 1970 a group of national health agencies gathered and found they had a common interest: the fate of patients with diseases so uncommon that they were not profitable for the drug manufacturers. There were therapies that had been developed to help these "orphans" but the drugs were not being manufactured and so were not available to the very people who needed them. Some patients were even dying for lack of the only drugs that could help them. Researchers were unable to garner sufficient grant funds to supply their studies. The industry tried to help but the costs of gaining FDA approval were too much for the companies to bear considering the great number of orphan drugs waiting for development. Because of the rarity of the diseases, each of the organizations involved represented too few constituents to have much clout with the FDA, so they joined forces to lobby for congressional action. Jack Klugman, star of television's forensic medicine series, *Quincy*, learned through his brother Maurice of their testimony before Congress and, in 1981, broadcast an episode of his popular show dealing with the orphan drug problem. National interest generated by this program nearly swamped the volunteers until NORD was incorporated as a nonprofit agency and was able to hire a part time staff. The fledgling organization continued to grow as more and more people made inquiries about increasingly rare disorders. A computer database has been set up and a networking program links patients with the same disease with each other and with sources of help. A merger with the National Orphan Drug and Device Foundation, a group set up to fund medical research for rare disorders, allows both organizations to function more efficiently and more effectively. Over fifty agencies (including the National Sjögren's Syndrome Association) are served by this umbrella agency and countless individual members benefit directly and indirectly. In recent years, NORD has been influential in promoting the extension of the Orphan Drug Act and in stimulating the appropriation of funds for research as well as for increasing the awareness of the problem in general. [172]

---

[172]"What is NORD?" NORD Newsletter New Fairfield CT5: 1

Contact Addresses for Agencies

National Sjögren's Syndrome Association: 3201 W. Evans Drive, Phoenix AZ 85023 1(800) 395-NSSA {6772}

NORD: P. O. Box 8923, New Fairfield, CT 06812-1783 (203) 746-6518 1 (800) 999-6673

Arthritis Foundation: 1314 Spring St., N. W., Atlanta, GA 30309 (404) 872-7100

Bay Area Lupus Foundation: 2635 North First Street, Suite #206, San Jose CA 95134 (408) 954-8600, 1-(800) 523-3363 FAX (408) 954-8129

British Sjögren's Syndrome Association: % Madeline Ford, 20 Kingston Way, Nailsea, Bristol, B S19 2RA, England

CFIDS Association of America,(chronic fatigue and immune dysfunction syndrome) PO Box 220398, Charlotte NC 28222-0398 (800) 442-3437, (900) 988-2343, FAX (704)365-9755

Fibromyalgia Association of Central Ohio, 3545 Olentangy River Road, Suite 088, COLUMBUS OH 43214 (614) 262-2000

Fibromyalgia Network, 5700 Stockdale Hwy., Suite 100, Bakersfield CA 93309 (805) 631-1950

Lupus Foundation of America: 4 Research Place, Suite 180, Rockville MD 20850-3226 (301) 670-9292 (800) 558-0121

Muscular Dystrophy Association: (Includes myositis and dermatomyositis among its multiple muscular disorder concerns): 810 Seventh Ave., New York NY 10019 (212) 586-0808

Scleroderma Federation:, Hdq Peabody Office Building, One Newberry Street Peabody MA 01960 (508) 535-0666, 1 (800) 422-1113, FAX (508) 535-6696

Sjögren's Syndrome Foundation: 382 Main Street, Port Washington, NY 11050 (516) 767-2866

United Scleroderma Foundation, Inc.: P.O.Box 399, Watsonville, CA 95077-0399 (408) 728-2202, 1-(800) 722-HOPE

Appendix II - Glossary of Terms Related to Sjögren's Syndrome

Achlorhydria - lack of hydrochloric acid in gastric juice

Acupressure - compression of muscles or connective tissue by means of needles

Acupuncture - technique for treating pain by inserting needles into specific parts of the body

Adenopathy - swelling of lymph nodes

Adrenal glands - supply hormones such as cortisone, estrogen, progesterone, and androgen

Alzheimer's disease - progressive brain disease characterized by premature deterioration of intellectual function

ANA - antinuclear antibody, a marker for autoimmune diseases such as lupus, Sjögren's syndrome, and scleroderma

Androgen - male hormone

Anti-La/SS-B antibody - found in serum of primary SS patients

Anti-Ro/SS-A antibody - found in serum of primary SS patients

Antibody - protein substance developed by the body to counteract a specific antigen

Antigen - Foreign substance, such as virus, toxin or bacteria which stimulates the immune system to produce antibodies

Artificial tears - drops designed to replace natural tears

Autoimmune disease - disorder in which the body's immune system reacts against healthy tissue

B cells - specialized lymphocyte (white blood cell) formed in bone marrow to produce antibodies

Biopsy - removal of a small piece of tissue to be studied microscopically

Bolus - a moistened ball of chewed food

Bone marrow - soft organic material filling bone cavities

Break up time (BUT) - test to measure quality of tear film on eye

Bromhexine - (Bisolvon) experimental drug to increase production of saliva, tears, and bronchial secretions

Bronchitis - inflammation of mucous membranes of the bronchial tubes

Candidiasis - a form of yeast infection attacking skin or mucous membranes

Caries - dental cavities

Carpal tunnel syndrome - a tenderness and weakness of the thumb caused by pressure on a nerve at the wrist.

Cellular immunity - the mechanical process of warding off foreign substances by white cells

Central Nervous System (CNS) - brain and spinal cord

Chyme - ball of semi-digested food as it progress through stomach and intestines

Cheilitis -(angular) cracking at corners of mouth often due to candidiasis

Cirrhosis - a chronic, degenerative disease of the liver

Conjunctivitis - inflammation of the mucous membrane lining the eyelids

Connective tissue - supports and connects other tissues and body parts

Connective tissue disease (CTD) - disorders characterized by inflammation of connective tissues and blood vessels (includes lupus, scleroderma, polymyositis, dermatomyositis, and polyarteritis) Also see Autoimmune disease

Cornea - transparent, multi-layered protective covering of the eye's pupil and iris

Corticosteroid - hormones produced by the adrenal glands

Cricoid cartilage - ring-like cartilage at lower part of larynx

Cytokine - a non-antibody protein that acts like an antibody.

Cytotoxic drugs - chemicals that destroy cells, used as anti-cancer drugs when specific for fast growing cells

Dermatomyositis - chronic disease characterized by inflammation of the muscles and skin

Dilatation (dilation) - expansion of an organ, opening, or duct

Diverticulitis - inflammation of sacs in the lining of the intestines and colon

Dysphagia - difficulty in swallowing

Dyspnea - difficulty in breathing

Dysfunction - abnormal or impaired action

Dysmotility - lacking the ability to make normal involuntary motions

Efamol - trade name for oil of evening primrose, experimentally used in treatment of SS

Electron microscope - uses a stream of electrons for greatly magnified images of objects

Enzymes - proteins that induce chemical changes in other substances without being changed themselves, i.e.; in digestive juices they are capable of breaking down foods into compounds usable by the body

Epistaxis - nosebleed

Epithelial cells - form the outer layer of the body and the linings of cavities

Erythrocyte - mature red blood cell

Erythema - red color in inflamed area

Esophagus - muscular tube carrying food from pharynx to stomach

Estrogen - female sex hormone

Etiology - causes of disease

Eustachian tube - leads from middle ear to pharynx, lined with mucous membrane

Evening primrose oil - see Efamol

Exocrine glands - glands whose secretions reach and lubricate the skin or mucous membranes

Extra-glandular - outside of, or in addition to, glands

Fatty acid - acids important to the digestive process

Fibromyalgia - arthritis-like condition causing muscle and tendon pain at specific points of the body

Fibrosis - abnormal formation, thickening or stiffening of fibrous tissues

Filamentary keratitis - inflammation of the cornea with stringy strands of epithelial cells

Flare - an increase in symptoms; as in 'flare up'

Fluorescein dye - used in testing for damage to cornea

Fluoride - a mineral commonly applied topically to teeth for prevention of decay

Gamma-linolenic acid - a fatty acid

Gastric glands - tubular glands in the mucous lining of the stomach

Glossitis - inflammation of the tongue

Goiter - an enlargement of the thyroid gland

Gold salts - injections used in treatment of rheumatoid arthritis or lupus

Gougerot's syndrome - a general condition in which the eyes, mouth, larynx, nose, and vulva all suffered from a related dryness which also affected the thyroid and ovaries. Described by the French physician, Dr. H. Gougerot.

Gynecologist - a specialist in diseases of the female reproductive system

Helper T cells - specialized lymphocytes designed to modulate the immune system

Hepatitis - a disorder characterized by inflammation of the liver

HLA - human leukocyte antigen

Humoral immunity - chemical immune action initiated by B cells producing antibodies in the blood serum

Hydrochloric acid - an ingredient of digestive juice

Hypotonic - a solution of lower osmotic pressure than another

IgA - an immunoglobulin

Immune system - organs and cells of the body involved in producing immune reactions

Immune tolerance - an immune cell's ability to know when *not* to react violently to another substance

Immunity - the ability to resist or overcome infections

Immunoglobulins - proteins capable of acting as antibodies

Immunosuppressive drugs - substances that interfere with the normal immune response. Protect foreign tissue grafts and combat autoimmune diseases

Indocin - a non-steroidal anti-inflammatory drug

Inflammation - tissue reaction to injury marked by redness, soreness, heat, swelling, or in SS, a concentration of lymphocytes

Internist - a specialist in diseases of the internal organs.

Interstitial cystitis - inflammation of the lining of the bladder

Interstitial nephritis - inflammation of connective tissue of kidneys

Keratoconjunctivitis sicca (KCS) - a condition of dry eyes caused by lymphocytic infiltration of the tear glands

Killer T cells - specialized lymphocytes which destroy invading foreign substances

Lacrimal glands - secrete tears to lubricate the eyes

Lactoferrin - protein found in tears and saliva

Lagophthalmos, nocturnal - incomplete closure of the eyelids during sleep

Larynx - upper end of the throat, a cartilage structure lined with mucous membrane, "voice box"

Lip (labial) biopsy - the taking of minor salivary glands from the lower lip as a diagnostic test for Sjögren's syndrome.

Liver - organ which secretes bile and contributes to metabolic functions, is main site for production of plasma proteins

Lymphocytes - white blood cells forming "soldiers" of the immune system

Lymphoma - malignant cell growth in lymph system

Masticate - to chew

Marker - gene or trait that identifies linked traits

Mixed connective tissue disease (MCTD) - a combination of four different autoimmune disorders

Meibomian glands - tear glands located in the eyelids

Mikulicz' disease - disorder described by Dr. Johann von Mikulicz-Radecki involving sicca syndrome. Later determined to be identical to Sjögren's syndrome.

Mucolytic agent - medication or spray which liquefies mucus

Mucous membranes - lining of passages and cavities communicating with the air, usually containing mucus secreting glands

Mucus - thick fluid secreted by mucous membranes and glands

Myositis - inflammation of the muscles

Natural killer (NK) cells - white cells programmed to destroy 'invaders'

Nervous System - network of nerve cells which coordinates body activity and receives and responds to stimuli.

Neonatal lupus erythematosus (NLE) - lupus-like symptoms seen in infants born to women with SS markers

Neuropathy - any disease of the nerves; in SS may produce tingling, burning or numbness of the skin

Nodule - small aggregation of cells sometimes seen under the skin in immune system disorders, also normal structural unit of lymph tissue

Non-steroidal anti-inflammatory drugs (NSAIDs) - drugs which reduce inflammatory response and pain

Nystatin suspension - antibiotic against fungus infections

Ophthalmologist - physician specializing in diseases and treatments of the eye

Oral mucosa - mucus membrane lining of the mouth

Oropharynx - the middle portion of the larynx

Osmotic pressure - tension between two solutions of different concentrations separated by a semipermeable membrane

Otitis - inflammation of the ear

Otolaryngologist - physician specializing in problems of the ear, nose and throat

Pancreas - digestive system gland that produces insulin for the metabolism of carbohydrates plus digestive pancreatic juice

Pancreatitis - inflammation of the pancreas

Parkinson's disease (PD) - chronic nervous disorder characterized by tremor, muscular weakness, and rigidity caused by a deficiency in the brain's production of the chemical dopamine

Parotid gland - major salivary gland located in front of the ear

Penicillamine - disease modifying medication used in treatment of rheumatoid arthritis and other autoimmune disorders

Peripheral nervous system (PNS) - nerve cell network outside of brain and spinal cord

Phagocyte - white cell that destroys foreign particles by literally 'eating' them

Pharynx - passageway for air from nasal cavity to larynx and for food from mouth to esophagus

Physiologic - having to do with body functions

Pilocarpine - drug used to stimulate saliva production.

Photosensitivity - reaction to light

Plaque - gummy mass of micro-organisms that grows on teeth and promotes decay

Pleurisy - inflammation of the membrane that surrounds the lungs

Pneumonia - inflammation in the lungs

Polyarteritis - inflammation of the medium and small arteries

Polymyositis - autoimmune disorder characterized by inflammation and degeneration of the muscles including weakness and muscle pain

Prednisone - a steroid hormone produced by the adrenal glands

Primary Sjögren's syndrome - inflammatory disorder affecting the exocrine glands and possibly involving multiple organ systems in the absence of another autoimmune disorder

Prostaglandins - fatty acid derivatives present in and affecting many tissues including the brain, lung, kidney, thymus, and pancreas

Psuedolymphoma - clusters of non-malignant cells giving the false appearance of true lymphomas

Puncta - ducts which drain excess tears into nasal cavity

Punctal occlusion - procedure to block puncta, retaining tears in eye

Purpura - red to purple areas under the skin caused by hemorrhages of small blood vessels usually found on the legs in SS

Raynaud's phenomenon - condition where the fingers (or toes and tip of nose) become very sensitive to cold, heat, or emotional stress, characterized by color changes from white to blue to red

Reflux - backing up of fluids and food from the stomach to the esophagus

Remission - lessening or temporary disappearance of symptoms with or without medication

Rheumatoid arthritis (RA) - autoimmune disorder characterized by inflammation of multiple joints including pain, stiffness, and swelling

Rheumatoid factor - immunoglobulin present in serum of eighty percent of adults with rheumatoid arthritis

Rheumatologist - physician who specializes in rheumatic diseases

Rhinitis - inflammation of the nasal lining

Rose bengal dye - used to detect damage to dry eye

Salicylates - aspirin-like drugs

Saline - salty

Salivary ducts - tubes connecting salivary glands to mouth

Salivary glands - glands which secrete fluids to lubricate and protect mouth

Schirmer test - used to measure secretion of tears with filter paper strip

Scintiscan - method of measuring fluids using radioactive substances

Scleroderma - chronic autoimmune disorder characterized by fibrosis of the skin and organs of the gastrointestinal tract, lungs, heart and kidneys.

Secondary Sjögren's syndrome - sicca (dry) symptoms experienced in combination with an underlying autoimmune disorder

Sed rate (erythrocyte sedimentation rate) - test of the speed at which erythrocytes settle in the blood, used to indicate presence of inflammatory disease

Sialogram - record of examination of salivary glands with X rays

Sicca complex - related symptoms of dry eyes and dry mouth

Sjögren's syndrome (SS) - a chronic systemic autoimmune disorder characterized by dryness of many areas of the body, most commonly the eyes and mouth and joints

Slit lamp - lamp constructed so that an intense light is emitted through a slit for the examination of the eye

Smooth muscle - muscle that carries out involuntary motions

Spleen - organ of lymph tissue for the production and storage of blood cells and blood filtration

SS-A (Anti-Ro),SS-B (Anti-La) - antibody markers for Sjögren's syndrome (although not unique to SS)

Steroids - hormones produced in the adrenal glands

Stomatitis - irritation of the lining of the mouth

Sublingual glands - salivary glands under the tongue

Submandibular glands - salivary glands lower jaw

Submaxillary glands - salivary glands in floor of mouth

Suppressor T cells - lymphocytes geared to inhibit the action of other lymphocytes and macrophages

Synovial capsule - enclosure formed by synovial membrane around joint

Synovial membrane - membrane enclosing the lubricating fluid of a joint

Synovitis - inflammation of the synovial membrane

Systemic - pertaining to the whole body, rather than one of its parts

Systemic lupus erythematosus (SLE or lupus) - chronic inflammatory autoimmune disorder affecting the skin, joints, kidneys, nervous system, and mucous membranes, characterized by immune complex deposition

T cells - lymphocytes (white blood cells) developed in the thymus programmed to alert immune system, destroy invading foreign cells and control antibody forming action of B cells

Thrush - infection of the tissues of the mouth and throat; a form of candidiasis

Thyroiditis - inflammation of the thyroid gland

Trans mandibular joint (TMJ) - joint connecting lower jaw to skull

Transient ischemic attacks (Ties) - temporary interference with blood supply to brain.

Trigeminal nerve - a facial nerve with three branches supplying sensation to eyes, skin, nasal cavities, gums, teeth and tongue and motor power for chewing.

Vaginitis - inflammation of the vagina

Van Bijsterveld score - dry eye measure using rose bengal staining

Vasculitis - inflammation of the blood vessels

Vitreous body - jelly-like substance filling the cavity of the eyeball

Waldenstrom's macroglobulinemia - disorder characterized by excessive production of immunoglobulins causing anemia, lassitude, confusion, and bleeding

Xerophthalmia - dryness of the eyes

Xerostomia - dryness of the mouth

Appendix IV - References

Arthritis Foundation. 1983. *Polymyositis and Dermatomyositis.* Atlanta GA: AF

Arthritis Foundation. 1983. *Rheumatoid Arthritis.* Atlanta GA: AF

Arthritis Foundation. 1983. *Scleroderma.* Atlanta GA: AF

Arthritis Foundation. 1984. *Systemic Lupus Erythematosus* Atlanta GA: AF

Berson, D. and Ray, S. 1978. *Pain Free Arthritis* Brooklyn NY: S & J Books

Daniels, T. E. and Talal, N. Eds. 1987. *Sjögren's Syndrome: Clinical and Immunological Aspects.* Berlin: Springer-Verlag

Dereiko, M. and Teutsch, E. *Recipes for Easy Chewing and Safe Swallowing.* Portland, OR: Dereiko-Teutsch & Associates

Dorros, S. 1981. *Parkinson's: A Patient's View.* Cabin John, MD: Seven Locks Press

Dorros, S. and Dorros, D. 1992. *Patient Perspectives on Parkinson's.* Miami: National Parkinson Foundation

Consumer Reports Books. eds. 1980. *Consumer's Union's Report on Fake Health Claims, Worthless Remedies, and Unproved Therapies.* Mt. Vernon NY: Consumer's Union

Fox, R. ed. 1992. *Rheumatic Clinics of America: Sjögren's Syndrome, Vol. 18, Number 3.* Philadelphia: W. B. Saunders Company

Fries, J. 1979. *Arthritis: A Comprehensive Guide.* Reading, MA: Addison-Wesley Publishing Company

Harris, K. ed. 1989. *The Sjogren's Syndrome Handbook.* New York: The Sjogren's Syndrome Foundation

Jameson, E. 1961. The *Natural History of Quackery*. Springfield IL: Charles C Thomas Publishers

Lewis, K. 1985. *Successful Living with Chronic Illness*. Wayne NJ: Avery Publishing Group

Lorig, K. and Fries, J. 1980. *The Arthritis Helpbook*. Reading, MA: Addison-Wesley Publishing Company

Michlovitz F. A., ed. 1990. *Thermal Agents in Rehabilitation*. Philadelphia: Davis Company

Mizel, S. and Jaret, P. 1985. *In Self Defense*. New York: Harcourt Brace Jovanovich, Publishers

National Cancer Institute 1987. *Eating Hints: Recipes and Tips for Better Nutrition During Cancer Treatment*. NIH Publication #87-2079. Bethesda MD: NIH

National Institute of Dental Research *Dry Mouth (Xerostomia.)* Pamphlet Bethesda MD

National Sjögren's Syndrome Association 1993. *Living Well With Sjögren's Syndrome*. Video. NSSA

Phillips, R. H. 1984. *Coping with Lupus*. Wayne, NJ: Avery Publishing Group Inc.

Pitzele, S. K. 1986. *We Are Not Alone: Learning to Live With Chronic Illness*. New York: Workman Publishing

Saathoff, M. A. 1991. *Fibromyalgia*. Fibromyalgia Association of Central Ohio

Shearn, M. 1971. *Sjögren's Syndrome*. Philadelphia: W. B. Saunders Company

Talal, N. ed. 1989. *Sjögren's Syndrome: A Model for Understanding Autoimmunity*. London: Academic Press Limited

Index

Comments from readers of

Sjögren's Syndrome: The Sneaky "Arthritis":

"Very informative." "I enjoyed the humor, direct approach, organized research." "An expert survey of SS." "Your book has brought me comfort."

"Enthralling, and just what is needed to spread the word."

Need extra copies for friends and family? Order below:

UNDERSTANDING SJÖGREN'S SYNDROME

Other books by the author:

Parkinson's Disease: The Mystery, The Search And The Promise
    Send ____copies @ $16.95 (FL $.90 tax) Postpaid
Sjögren's Syndrome: The Sneaky "Arthritis" (out of print)
Sjögren's Syndrome: The Sneaky "Arthritis" Japanese Edition
Houston By Stages: a History of Theatre in Houston
    Send ____copies @ $29.95 (FL $1.80 tax)Postpaid

Yes! Please send me _____ copies of *Understanding* Sjögren's Syndrome @ $18.95 ea., Postpaid. (Florida residents add $1.02 sales Tax.) North America: US $19.50 Other locations: US$21.50 (add US $6.00 for airmail) Make check payable to Pixel Press
Mail to: Pixel Press
             Dept. B
             PO Box 3151
             Tequesta FL 33469

Name:_____

Street:_____

City:_____St____ZIP_____